LIFELINES

EDITED B

THE

WI
Cl

S. Brockhurst

LIFELINES

EDITED BY CHRIS GIDNEY

THE STORY OF
WENDY CRAIG

Marshall Pickering
An Imprint of HarperCollinsPublishers

Marshall Pickering is an Imprint of HarperCollins*Religious*
part of HarperCollins*Publishers*
77–85 Fulham Palace Road, London w6 8jb
www.christian-publishing.com

First published in Great Britain in 1999
by HarperCollins*Publishers*

10 9 8 7 6 5 4 3 2 1

A catalogue record for this book
is available from the British Library

ISBN 0 551 03210 3

Printed and bound in Great Britain by
Caledonian International Book Manufacturing Ltd, Glasgow

"Reading about the life of Jesus Christ is certainly one of the most fascinating, exciting and challenging journeys you could ever make," says Wendy Craig.

She has starred in such classic TV series as *Not in Front of the Children*, *And Mother Makes Three* and the much-acclaimed *Butterflies*, all of which are now being shown on TV for a new generation to enjoy. Wendy Craig is still everybody's favourite TV mum.

Many of the characters that she has played over the years have been rather incompetent and scatter-brained, but the real-life Wendy is quite different – although she admits that she can be a bit forgetful. She jokingly puts her absent-mindedness down to her age. Some of her characters were totally unable to produce anything edible from the oven, but Wendy is quite anxious to point out that in real life she does know how to cook! "I could do the Sunday lunch by the time I was about 12," she proudly recalls, remembering that her mother taught her all the basics.

An accomplished actress, Wendy is also a writer, having penned many of the episodes of the sequel *And*

Mother Makes Five with her husband, Jack Bentley. The BBC peak-hour drama series *Nanny* was also based on her own idea and formulation. Whilst travelling to visit her mother one day, she had hurriedly bought a women's magazine from the platform bookstall just as the train was leaving, and she settled down to read it as the train pulled away from the station. She noticed that at the back of the magazine there were a lot of adverts for the position of nanny, and she thought this would make an ideal subject for a television play.

Deciding to research her idea at the local library, she was surprised at how much information was available. Realizing that there was enough material to fill a whole TV series, she wrote a suggested format and sent it to the BBC under a pseudonym. "I thought that if they saw it was from Wendy Craig they would think I was just trying to get myself another job!" she explains. "My agent rang me about three months later and said the BBC wanted to do the series, but they wanted to meet the author! Then I was terrified that they wouldn't let me play the part!" They did, of course, and it soon became a successful series.

However, Wendy's writing is not restricted to television plays. She has written several books, including two "Busy Mum's Cook Books" for children, which became best-sellers. She has also won a gold disc for her recorded version of *The Tales of Beatrix Potter*.

Wendy is one of those rare actresses who can play almost any role, from classic parts to pantomime. Kenneth Tynan once described her as "one of the six best young actresses in the Western world". Her professional biography is very extensive, and the list of her awards shows that she is loved and esteemed by many people in her profession and by the general public. She has been voted "Actress of the Year", "BBC Personality of the Year", "BBC TV's Woman of the Year" and also "The Funniest Woman on Television" for three years running.

Family life

If her two teenage sons were embarrassed by the latter award at the time, they never showed it, though one can imagine that they got a fair ribbing at school!

Family life for Wendy has always been something that she has been anxious about. Juggling a highly successful career whilst desiring to be an equally successful mum at home had its problems. "I just had to be extremely well organized," she explains. "I was not an absent parent, though, and I was fortunate in my working schedule, as I used to rehearse the programmes in the mornings and was supposed to go home and learn my lines in the afternoons. This meant that I was always there when the boys came home from school, and was always able to put them to bed, and was there again in the morning when they woke up. I was never away on tour or location for any length of time either. It was like being a mum who was a part-timer."

Childhood faith

God has not always played a central part in Wendy's life. "When I was a little girl I had a very strong faith," she recalls, "though, sadly, I gradually squeezed God out of my life as I got older." She grew up in a mining village in County Durham. She describes it as a lovely place to be, as the people were very kind to each other, as they often are in areas of hardship. Her grandparents lived with Wendy and her parents. Her grandmother had been a teacher, but had now lost her sight. Although incapacitated, she was a true believer in Christ, and Wendy cannot recall ever seeing her unhappy. Wendy loved being with her grandmother and would often creep into her room at the back of the house, into an atmosphere that she describes as "a haven of peace".

Wendy would sit transfixed at her feet, listening to all the Bible stories, hymns and parables of Jesus that Grandma would recall from her seemingly endless memory. Wendy's Christian faith and understanding of Jesus grew out of the love and respect that she had for her grandmother, and she remembers those early years with great fondness.

Her parents then sent her to a Church of England school where, Wendy says, the Christian teachers "lived their faith". When she was a little child Wendy's faith was strong. She really believed that she could trust God. She says, "In my simple way, I loved him."

When the family moved to live on a farm, Wendy became acutely aware of creation and of God as the Creator. She was the sort of child who enjoyed solitude, and she spent a lot of time sitting or walking alone in the glorious countryside, taking in the air, appreciating the views and feeling a strong awareness of God's presence. "I felt extremely uplifted living there," she says. "I could really feel the power and goodness of God surround me. I never felt I was alone."

Years of youthful dreams came true when Wendy was offered a place at a London drama school. She was then able to see plays in the West End and to mix with like-minded people who shared her passion for the theatre. It was all very exciting, but as her career progressed she began to drift away from her Christian faith.

Marriage and family life also kept her busy and distanced her from anything spiritual. Wendy says her life seemed to run like clockwork. "Life was so full, and I actually began to think that I could do it all myself.

I even started to believe that all the Bible stories my grandmother had taught me were just some sort of children's myth – sweet, but totally irrelevant to my everyday existence. Surely I didn't need God, anyway – I could live my life as I wanted to. In the end I quite simply walked away from God." Any thoughts of God and church were drowned out for the next 20 years, as she lived for her children, her husband and her career.

An emptiness inside

As Wendy was approaching her fortieth year, and despite being in the middle of a highly successful acting career, she began to feel a sort of emptiness inside, as though something was missing. She brushed off these feelings with excuses about her age, but the constant void remained, and she felt uncomfortable even at the best of times. These feelings that gnawed away inside her eventually started to unnerve her, but she felt unable to do anything about them. She says the Lord himself brought these feelings to a head when a personal tragedy struck her.

Wendy feels that this story will sound a bit sentimental, but she knows that God uses all sorts of experiences to bring us to him. "I had a lovely old English Setter, and we used to walk together in the countryside near our home in Berkshire. One night I could hear my dog trying to get up the stairs, so I got out of bed to help him – just in time to see him crumple and fall down again. I realized that he was dying. He was an old dog, and although I knew that big dogs like mine didn't live very long anyway, I was absolutely appalled. I held him in my arms, and he died a few moments later with a great shudder.

"I was quite shocked because I really loved him. I began to mourn for my dog, missing him so very much, and I found that I couldn't stop grieving for him. I couldn't eat, couldn't sleep and didn't want to go anywhere. My unhappiness and sense of loss overshadowed every part of my life. Everything seemed to become less important than my grief, and I slowly slid into a deep depression."

The family were all very supportive, offering to buy her another dog, but Wendy knew that it wasn't just the dog. "I recognized that it was that strange emptiness within that had finally boiled up like a huge tumour inside me. I would constantly try to analyse this feeling, until I sat down in the garden one day and asked God if he would please tell me what was going on." She admitted that she had not used the words "Please, God" for a very long time, and it was at that moment that she realized that when she had been out walking with her dog she had been reliving the wonderful peace and nearness to God that she had experienced as a child on the farm.

Wendy knew that she needed to get back to her childhood faith. Getting into her car, she drove straight to her local church and sat down in one of the empty seats. She asked God to forgive her for turning her back on him and asked if he would have her back. She remembers that from that moment "all that sadness and misery just dropped away. It was like a reassuring hand on my shoulder, and all my pain dissolved. I knew I'd been forgiven. I felt like a new person, and I knew that I had been reborn into Christ's family."

Wendy smiles as she remembers God's perfect timing. A couple of days later, when she was on her way to the local butcher's and was feeling in need of someone to talk to about her rediscovered faith, she literally bumped into a lady she had never met before. "We got talking, and she suddenly invited me to a local meeting where women discussed the Christian faith. She said they met on a Wednesday morning to pray for and support each other. I knew that six months ago I would have politely brushed her off as quickly as possible, but I knew that this was just what I now needed."

Wendy felt a little overwhelmed by all the lost years that she somehow had to make up, and by all the things that she apparently had to re-learn. The years of not reading her Bible, not praying, not spending time with other Christians, and not talking to a loving Heavenly Father whom she knew was longing to talk to her – all this began to be sorted out as she attended the meetings and experienced the beginning of a new life. Even her friends in the acting business noticed a difference. One actress asked her outright why she had lost the intense, driving ambition that she had always displayed. Wendy appreciated her friend's honesty and explained to her that her Christian faith had been rekindled and that she had begun a new chapter in her life. This was to be Wendy's first opportunity to lead someone to God, as a few weeks later her friend made her own commitment to Christ.

A shared faith

Wendy was married to the musician and journalist Jack Bentley for 39 years. They had two sons – Alastair, who is now an oboist with the Birmingham Royal Ballet, and Ross, who is a writer. Wendy tragically lost Jack in 1994, soon after she had regained her Christian faith. She still misses him, and describes her marriage as wonderfully supportive, despite the fact that he did not embrace her new faith. In fact he was a confirmed atheist, but Wendy often prayed that one day they would be able to share a faith in Christ. A kind and loving man, Jack was also strong and self-sufficient, able to cope with life on his own terms, and he felt that he really had no need of God.

When he became seriously ill, Wendy invited some Christian friends to come and pray in her house. They spoke to Jack very gently about God's love and offered to pray for him, but he refused. Becoming hospitalized soon afterwards, he was approached by a little Filipino nurse, who asked if he would allow her to pray for him. Again he declined. The nurse was not to be put off, however, and she insisted that she and Wendy should pray, even if he didn't want them to. "Three days later I was visiting Jack, when he suddenly sat up in bed and asked for all the nurses to come into his room. We all stood around the bed and he said, 'I want to tell you that I've become a Christian.' I just couldn't believe it!" Wendy was overjoyed.

Jack became increasingly unwell, but Wendy was comforted by the sense of peace that surrounded her husband. Sadly, he died a few weeks later. "My grief was tempered with the knowledge that he was safely with Jesus," says Wendy. "It gave me the certainty that I will meet him again one day. I look forward to that."

Words are important to any actress. Wendy still loves to write, and she has compiled a personal collection of poems and songs. One song, "Show me the Way", came to her while she was walking in her beloved countryside, praying for guidance soon after Jack's death. She says, "When I got home I could still remember it, so I sang it onto a tape and a friend arranged it for me." These are the song's words:

When I'm confused, Lord, show me the way.
Show me, show me, show me the way.
Baffled and bruised, Lord, show me the way.
Show me, show me, show me the way.

Still my heart and heal my mind,
Repair my soul to hear
Your still, small voice,
Your word of truth.
Peace, be still, your Lord is here.
Always so close to show you the way,
Show you, show you, show you the way.

When I'm afraid, Lord, show me the way.
Show me, show me, show me the way.
Grief and dismay, Lord, show me the way.
Show me, show me, show me the way.

Lift my spirit with your love,
Bring courage, hope and peace,
You who bore all for my sake
So I could walk from fear released.
With you beside me, showing the way,
Showing, showing, showing the way.

Spiritual food

The Bible now became Wendy's spiritual food, vital to her growth as a Christian. She has been strengthened, guided and enlightened by God's word countless times in many different situations. One Bible verse that is especially important to her is Zephaniah 3:17, which says:

> The LORD your God is with you;
> his power gives you victory.
> The LORD will take delight in you,
> and in his love he will give you new life.
> He will sing and be joyful over you.

Wendy says that, in common with a lot of actors, she is not the most confident person in the world. "I am so often filled with doubt – doubt of every kind, including self-doubt, as well as doubt about my faith," she admits. "Many times I have stood in the wings, at the side of the stage, before making my entrance, filled with terror and convinced that I'd never get through the show. But the scriptures always have a word to help us, if we care to look. When I saw this verse, it leapt out at me. It was just what I needed to hear at that moment. Here was the reassurance I was seeking."

Wendy says that when you discover that you are loved by someone, it's a terrific boost to your confidence. Knowing that you are loved by God is the greatest confidence boost of all. "So now, whenever doubt and dread besiege me – which they inevitably do – instead of collapsing like a wimp, I whisper Zephaniah 3:17 to myself, and, having absorbed the power of these words, I stand tall. It really works!"

Mark's Gospel is also important to Wendy. She describes it as an easy-to-read introduction to the life of Jesus, but she emphasizes that it's important to read Matthew, Luke and John as well, because that will give you a complete picture of what Jesus was like, as each author gives his own angle. The authors wrote for different audiences. Matthew's Gospel was for the Jews, while Mark's version was for the Christians who lived in Rome. "It's an exciting account, giving a straightforward, energetic commentary," says Wendy. "It focuses more on events than on what was said. That's why I like it. I don't get bogged down in theology by reading Mark, and it relates to me, now, here, today – and that's vital!"

Wendy always tries to make time to regularly read her Bible. She sees the daily digestion of scripture as an essential part of her life. "I set my alarm to allow myself half an hour to read and pray before I get up each morning. I use Bible notes to help me choose a passage, and it gives me the grounding I need for each day I face. Reading the Bible teaches me so much and definitely brings me closer to God.

"I also wake up in the night a lot, and I find it very difficult to get back to sleep. I'm so awake then that I could get up and do the ironing! It's very annoying, because I end up feeling very tired the next day. One day I thought that maybe God wanted me to use this wakeful time, so when it happens I have got into the habit of picking up my Bible or praying. I have felt on occasions that God possibly wanted me to pray for someone specific, so I lie there and pray for people who come into my mind, and soon afterwards I drift off to sleep again."

Wendy finds herself trying to listen to God more and more, as she relies on him so much, although she admits that her own will gets in the way a lot of the time. She also concedes that she sometimes has a bit of a struggle on her hands when she wants to do something but feels that God doesn't approve. This can make her feel very torn, but she is comforted by the knowledge that God has her best interests at heart.

Although she enjoys any opportunity to read her Bible, Wendy confesses that she is not very good at remembering passages and where they came from. "I suppose I should spend some more time learning Bible passages parrot-fashion. The thing is, when I read the

Bible these days, sometimes a passage will really jump out at me. When that happens I write it down in a little book that I carry around with me, so that I can draw strength from it when I need to.

"As an actress you spend a lot of time being frightened – about going out on stage, about forgetting your lines or making mistakes. You feel pretty insecure, and as you get older you feel more and more insecure because your memory is not as good as it was. Certain Bible passages are a real help to me, such as Mark 4:40, when Jesus says, 'Why are you frightened? Have you still no faith?' Then in Mark 6:50 he says, 'It is I. Don't be afraid!' In fact, the Bible has 366 references to people being told not to be afraid. That means one for every day of the year, and one for a leap year too! Obviously, God knows that I need to hear this. So how can you go on stage after reading a passage like that and still be afraid? You don't, because you take Jesus on stage with you."

Living out her faith

It isn't always easy to hold unswervingly to your beliefs while being constantly in the public's eye. Peer and work pressures abound, but Wendy is adamant that despite these difficulties, she would never deny her faith. However, she feels that it is not always appropriate to bring it up in every conversation. "The Lord lets you know the right time to speak and the right time to stay quiet," she believes. "In some instances you could go blazing in talking about Jesus, and instead of helping people, it would just make them withdraw. It would be counter-productive."

At work, Wendy will often simply stay quiet about her faith, until someone asks her about it because they have heard that she is a Christian. She believes that rather than forcing the door open herself, it is much better to wait for people to open the door themselves. She tries to live out her faith as best she can at work as well as at home. She admits that she often gets it wrong, but at least she tries to live as she believes God wants her to. Sometimes, when people are curious enough to ask about her faith, she gives them only a brief answer rather than diving in with a whole sermon! She then adds them to her private prayer list, and perhaps later, when she thinks they are ready to hear it, she will explain her faith more fully.

Her faith has influenced her working life in other ways too. There are certain roles that she would not be at all happy to play. However, that is not to say that she would never play a villain – it's fun to play a dastardly character, so long as they get their just deserts in the end. In a nutshell, Wendy would not play a part in which wickedness is glorified. It seems to her that many of the parts in television drama these days are like that.

Being used to different roles, Wendy is also keen to have a role in her local church, where she helps to run an "Alpha" course. The course gives people an opportunity to explore the Christian faith for themselves, without pressure or manipulation, and in a relaxed, fun atmosphere. Wendy feels that this is one way in which she can "give something back" to God. She describes her role as "menial" – she puts out the seats and helps cook the meal – but in fact she loves to discuss the many questions she is asked about her faith and her experience of God in her life. "Alpha" is especially for people who don't normally go to a church, and this excites Wendy enormously. "It's an opportunity for people to ask honest questions about the Christian faith, without feeling like a fool," she says.

The question that is asked most often is, "If God is a God of love, why does he allow so much suffering, and why doesn't he intervene?" Wendy says, "My answer is that we live in a fallen and dying world. There is a lot of trouble and sadness in the world that is caused not by God but by mankind's greediness. He weeps over it just as much as we do, and is always there alongside the suffering. He promises to help us through these times if we ask him to. Sometimes I have to admit that I don't have the answer, but that doesn't make my faith any less real.

I have to be content with the fact that if I knew all the answers I wouldn't need faith – I would be God himself!"

An accurate account

Mark's Gospel was written in about AD 65, and so is the earliest of the four Gospels. Since it was written only about 35 years after the death of Christ, Wendy feels confident that it is an accurate account of his life and ministry. Other historical manuscripts published even later after an event are still considered accurate and reliable by historians. There is also more documented evidence that Jesus lived on earth than there is proof that Julius Caesar really existed!

Mark was not an eye-witness of the events recorded in his Gospel, but the young man mentioned in Mark 14:51, when Jesus was in the process of being arrested, is assumed by many scholars to be Mark himself. Mark drew most of his information from the apostle Peter, who was one of Jesus' closest friends and was present at all the most significant incidents mentioned in the Gospel.

Mark is the shortest of the four Gospels, containing only 16 chapters. It is concise and full of action. The purpose of the Gospel is to show, in a simple and straightforward manner, that Jesus Christ was the Son of God. Wendy finds Mark's Gospel easy to read, since it does not use much theological jargon.

Some of the stories in Mark worry her, though – such as the one in Chapter 5 where the evil spirits are sent into the pigs. "That's just because I'm an animal lover and very soppy about them!" explains Wendy. "I can't bear to think of those poor swine having to rush down the hill and drown in the sea. I think pigs are rather endearing creatures, as I was brought up on a farm. I used to like watching their antics, especially the baby piglets. They always seemed to be contented with whatever they had.

"I am sad that in the Bible as a whole there seems to be little interest in animals. I expect that a lot of this has to do with the fact that animals were not seen as pets in biblical days. Maybe many of them were dangerous, and a dog bite could mean becoming very ill with rabies, for example. Most creatures were there to work and to be of practical use to their masters. You get the feeling that Jesus didn't seem to give much priority to nature either. I suppose that's because Jesus considered humanity more important than any other part of his creation. He was absolutely focused on human beings. Women and men obviously come first on his list of priorities. Not that this gives us the right to be cruel to other living things, of course. Creation has been given to us to enjoy.

"There are also parts of Mark's Gospel that I find hard to come to terms with. Mark 11:12 talks about the barren fig tree that Jesus cursed. Again, because I'm such a nature lover, it seems unbelievable to me that Jesus would do such a thing to his own creation. I hold God's world in great respect and awe, and I think that what he made is very beautiful, so I am sad that Jesus cursed the tree. But it was a symbol of God's people, the Jews, who should have been producing spiritual fruit, but were in fact barren. The symbol also applies to us today. It's no good saying we are Christians if we don't actually show something for it. God doesn't want us to live a 'religious' life without substance.

"When I come across a part of the Bible that I don't quite understand, I ask God to help me to see what he is saying through it. I want every part of God's word to make a difference in my life. I don't want to miss a thing."

As a writer and actress, Wendy finds that Mark's Gospel unfolds like a wonderful piece of drama, building up to an amazing climax at the end. The actor Alec McCowen became famous for acting out the whole of Mark's Gospel as a one-man show. It was extremely effective and successful, both on tour and in the West End of London at the Comedy Theatre. A local Christian group gave away a copy of Mark's Gospel to every person who came to see the show. Wendy is amazed that McCowen was able to memorize every single verse, word for word.

A dynamic character

There are many aspects of Jesus' life as recorded in this Gospel that Wendy feels she can relate to in a professional capacity. The whole idea of Jesus being able to engage the attention of so many people at once fascinates her. Incidents such as the feeding of the 5,000 show that Jesus was a dynamic character. He managed to keep the attention of the crowd all day long, in intense heat, on uncomfortable ground, without food (until he provided it!) and with children too.

"What he was saying must have been so interesting and must have fed them with all kinds of things that they really needed and wanted to hear," says Wendy. "He was a great communicator, which is what every performer is always striving to be. It always puzzles me how he managed to make himself heard in front of so many people. In the absence of amplifiers and microphones, I'm sure he relied on the natural amphitheatres of the day, whether he stood at the base of a semicircular valley or used a boat on Lake Galilee as a stage. I live at the top of a very steep hill which drops away down to a river, and we can often hear things that are happening in the village about a mile below us. The natural slope of the hill, assisted by the wind, just carries the sound up to us as if it came from the next-door field. Jesus still must have had great voice projection, however – that's something else that people in the acting profession really work hard for."

Wendy recognizes that Jesus was the greatest communicator of all time, and appreciates that he was a great storyteller with a very clever technique. His parables were interesting, vivid and related to the everyday life of the people he was talking to. He didn't so much preach at them as draw them into his way of thinking. Wendy says, "Despite the fact that many of his points were challenging and hard, somehow he had the ability to present his thoughts in such a way that people never felt alienated. He did a lot of travelling, just like me, and always had a full house – yet another experience that every actress longs for!"

Fame – a mixed blessing

One of the pitfalls of being a celebrity is the danger of being taken for granted. When you enter the homes of millions of people via television on a regular basis, people tend to see you as public property. Similarly, Jesus was very famous and there were times when he did not want anyone to know where he was. His fame was spreading rapidly and it was becoming more and more of a restriction on him. He could not go outside without a huge crowd gathering around him, and he did not want to become known as some sort of magician or faith healer. People's spiritual welfare was a greater priority for him than their physical health, and if he spent his whole time healing, he would have no time for anything else.

Fame would only get in the way of his mission. Wendy too has found that fame can get in the way of her personal life, but she takes comfort from the fact that, in her small way, she has experienced a problem that Jesus himself had to face. "Can you imagine the impact of a man going around laying hands on sick people, and then they get up and walk?!" she says. "No wonder there were thousands following his every move. I think another reason why Jesus had to hide away was that he got so tired. We seem to forget that as well as being God, he was also a human being. His was such a short ministry – just three years – and he packed so much into that brief period of his life. It must have seemed as if his work was non-stop, 24 hours a day. He must have become physically very weary at times, and he hid himself away so that he could get some rest."

At one time it was quite difficult for Wendy to get out and about without being constantly interrupted by people. Although it was wearisome to have her privacy taken away, she always tried to look upon it as a compliment. "Shopping was a particular problem," she says, "as people would always come up and ask questions or request an autograph. I always felt a bit silly signing my name on a scrap of paper when I was standing next to the frozen peas! People were generally very nice and kind, and it was often a pleasurable experience – it's just that it took so long for me to get the groceries!"

She found that the most burdensome moments were when the family wanted to be able to enjoy a quiet meal together in a restaurant. This was not really possible, and Jack and the boys found the interruptions irritating. Sometimes they didn't get a lot of peace when she was with them in public. One day she decided to do something about it, and actually went to great lengths to create some private time with her family. "We were on holiday in southern France, and although I was sure that no one would notice me so far from home, I decided that I would not take any chances. We were sitting on the veranda of a restaurant, enjoying some cheese and French bread, and I had covered my own short, fair hair with a long-haired brown wig and had put on a pair of sunglasses. Suddenly some English people drove by in an open-topped car and shouted across the street, 'Hello, Wendy! What you got that wig on for?!' We all doubled up in laughter, and I never tried to kid anybody else after that."

A hiding place

Wendy's beloved home in the Berkshire countryside is her hiding place from the public eye. Surrounded by fields and single-track roads, it is very secluded without being totally cut off. The house, which has been her family's home for more than 30 years, sits snugly at the top of a hill and has magnificent views over the surrounding area. Many of Wendy's poems and songs have been inspired by her walks in the local countryside.

"I am very often aware of God's presence. He becomes very real to me in ordinary situations, such as when I'm out walking the dog or in the supermarket or driving my car. It just comes upon me suddenly, and I feel an ecstatic sensation of being incredibly close to him. Often when I'm praying I really feel I get an answer – very straightforward, short and matter-of-fact. Yet the answer will be nothing that I could have thought of myself, and I just have to accept that it is probably from God. The things that really make me smile and remind me that he is a Father are the small things that he does – the little gifts, or the moments when something just works out perfectly. They make me say, 'Thank you very much! That's so kind. You really are there after all, and you know what's happening.' These moments are terribly precious and I always know they are from God, almost like little rewards."

The reality of Wendy's public life is never far away, however, and at a recent event to publicize the popular "Alpha" courses, she found herself in nearby Wokingham. Standing alongside the Bishop of Reading, she released some helium-filled balloons with the Alpha course telephone number printed on the side, and, as always, she smiled for the clutch of press photographers who had gathered to witness the event. A week later she was not surprised to see the newspaper headline, "The actress and the bishop". "Still, it got the point across!" she laughs.

She is well aware of her abilities as an actress but emphasizes that all talent is God-given. She has been given the talent to be an actress, while other people, for example, may have been given the talent to be musicians or teachers. The important thing is to use your talent when and where possible.

Yet despite all the accolades she has received over the years, it would be difficult to find a more humble actress. She often lacks self-confidence, and yet her doubts about her own ability only serve to enhance her humility and grace. Her deep faith in God and her steady reliance on him are obviously key elements in her life. Wendy is someone who knows her worth, and yet she is able to see that God is much bigger than she is.

Timing

In the theatre timing is everything. If you get the timing wrong, the laugh is lost. If your timing is right, the audience applauds. Timing was also crucial for Jesus in his mission on earth. He was always in great demand, and, of course, he had all the marks of being the Messiah. The Jews were expecting a political Messiah – someone who would help them to defeat the Romans, who were currently occupying their land. Wendy can see from Mark's Gospel that Jesus had to be careful to avoid being manipulated by other people, who might want to use him as a catalyst for a religious war against their enemies. He steered clear of political involvement and concentrated on the work that God had sent him to do. He made sure that he followed God's timing and not other people's.

"Sometimes I do feel pressurized a lot," Wendy says. "I feel duty bound to help whenever I can, because I am in a privileged position. It's a case of 'Here I am, Lord – send me!'" Wendy has an agent who filters all the commercial requests for her involvement, but she finds it hard to say "no" to invitations from Christian sources. "I know I do too much," she says, "sometimes driving around all over the place, and I'm aware that I could tire myself out to the point where I could become unwell and so be no use to anyone. But God means so much to me and he has changed my life so much that I really want to give something back. I know you can't 'owe' God anything, but I do feel that I want to somehow 'repay' him for all that he has done. I do try not to over-tire myself, but quite often I hear God say, 'For goodness' sake be still, Wendy!'"

Wendy finds it helpful to see how Jesus handled his fame. She notices that there is not one example of him being pushed around by anybody unless it was part of his plan. He always did what he felt was best and resisted being manipulated.

Just part of the crowd?

Not surprisingly, the many different women who appear in Mark's Gospel are significant figures for Wendy. She is particularly intrigued by the story in Chapter 5 in which a woman touched the back of Jesus' cloak. Being a woman, she finds this event very moving. "It amazes me that in all that crowd, Jesus knew that someone had touched him and really needed his help. There must have been so many people pressing in on him, and yet he was so sensitive to this woman's needs at that time. As on other occasions, his disciples tried to dissuade their master from bothering about it, asking him how he could ask such a silly question as 'Who touched my clothes?' Jesus insisted on knowing who had done it and was not prepared to continue until he had met the person concerned. Jesus must have thought, 'Hello, what's that? Someone must be really trying to reach me.'

"The poor lady had been healed the instant she had touched Jesus, and probably didn't want to bother him, intending to just slip back into the crowd. Yet she had not left the scene when Jesus looked around, and, trembling, she came and knelt before him. She had apparently spent every penny she had on trying to find a cure for her internal bleeding. She had been ill for 12 years, but all the doctors had only made her worse. The woman had amazing faith, and she must have used up all her energy trying to get near to Jesus, in order to touch him, trusting that she would be healed. She was, of course."

Wendy wants to have the faith and the trust to go to Jesus and ask him for what she needs, believing that she won't be turned away or laughed at, that Jesus won't say he's too busy for her at the moment or she's not important enough for his attention. It was reported a few years ago that most fathers spend an average of just 60 seconds per day on proper communication with their children. Wendy says that God, our heavenly Father, is ready to listen to us all the time. She feels that we take this fact too much for granted and easily lapse into ignoring him most of the time – until an emergency arises!

In this passage in Mark's Gospel, Jesus was on an emergency mission to visit a sick child. Jairus had made a strong plea that Jesus should come and heal his daughter. Yet on the way to Jairus' house, Jesus still had time to stop and talk to this woman. Despite the fact that Jesus knew that this delay would mean that Jairus' daughter would die before he got there, he still wanted to meet the woman (of course, he later brought the dead girl back to life). He had an extraordinary sense of timing and a wonderful compassion for others. He could not be rushed or persuaded against his will. He did things in his own way, and in his own time. He had total confidence in his own powers, and many other people were learning to have confidence in him too.

"Sometimes we feel that we're just part of the crowd," says Wendy. "How can Jesus be interested in me? He has all these other people who need him so much more. He really doesn't have time to consider my needs. I am just an ordinary person, going about my daily business. Why should Jesus be concerned about me? Why would he take delight in me – me, with my flat feet and squeaky voice! Yet this is exactly what happened here. Jesus showed that this woman was loved and cared for. He knows us not as people in a crowd but as individuals. He knows each one of us by name. He wraps me in his love and quietens my fears."

Female followers

Wendy is particularly intrigued by Mark 15:41, which says: "Many other women who had come to Jerusalem with him were there also." She comments, "At first sight one might be suspicious about Jesus' female followers. Indeed, it's sad that several films and books have tried to suggest that he had personal, close relationships with the women who surrounded him. I can't find anything in the Gospels to support such an idea, and the society that Jesus lived in was nothing like ours. I think it's wrong to try to fit our cultural ways onto the life of Jesus. It's clear that the women served him in terms of preparing food, washing his clothes and making sure that he was comfortable. From what I can see of Jesus, I reckon he had a real soft spot for women. He really understood them. It was a very male-dominated society, but he displayed tenderness and compassion to all the women he met. They were not used to being treated as equals, and I think they loved it and followed him so that they could be near him as much as possible. Their society put them down, but Jesus made them feel valued, respected and loved."

About the fact that more women than men attend church, Wendy comments, "I think women find it easier to commit themselves to the love of God than men do. Maybe men feel that by believing in God and having to admit their weaknesses they are emasculating themselves. Women don't see it in this way, and are simply able to accept that God understands their situation."

The God of the Bible is usually seen as an all-powerful, strong Father figure who can do mighty things, such as parting the Red Sea, but Wendy does not feel "second best" because she is a woman. She says, "I know I have my place in society as a woman, and I know that God understands me better than anyone else – even better than I know myself. That is a great comfort to me.

"There was a time when I had become a Christian but my husband Jack had not, and he was finding that very difficult to cope with. I discussed this problem with my friend Angie, who helped me to see what I had been doing. I had always turned to Jack for all my advice and help. He was the one I had relied on over so many years together. Now I was often on my knees to this mysterious person called Jesus, who was also a man. I would be reading my Bible regularly, taking note of what Jesus said, and I was now trying to follow him. I suddenly understood that Jack was feeling very jealous. This had never occurred to me before. So, whilst not compromising my faith, I found ways to help Jack feel less threatened."

The Bible shows us that God has both masculine and feminine qualities. Indeed, Genesis underlines the fact that man and woman were made in his image. In Mark's

Gospel, Jesus displays both tenderness and strength. The two went hand in hand in his life. "In the East," says Wendy, "they have a word for God that literally means 'the breasted one' – that is, a mother, the one you turn to for succour and comfort. There is a great sense of the maternal as well as the paternal about Jesus in Mark's Gospel, and this reflects what God is like too. I can go to God if I need comfort, guidance or protection."

Wendy understands that some people may find it difficult to relate to God as Father or Mother. "If you had a human parent who was cruel, ignored your needs and treated you badly, it is very hard to think of God as a parent. My prayer for those who are in this position is that as they walk hand in hand with God through their life's journey, they will discover what a good father and mother are really like. It really is a question of letting go, and of trusting. It can be a difficult task."

Another story about a woman with faith can be found in Mark 7:24–30. The Phoenician woman had begged Jesus to drive a demon out of her daughter. Jesus had wanted a quiet place in which to teach his disciples. Using imagery, Jesus answered her plea by saying, "Let us first feed the children [i.e. the Jews]. It isn't right to take the children's food and throw it to the dogs [i.e. non-Jews such as Phoenicians]." The woman then gave an incredibly clever answer, using the same imagery: "Sir, even the dogs under the table eat the children's leftovers!" This persistence obviously moved Jesus, and he granted her wish.

Wendy thinks this woman was very bright and very daring to approach Jesus in this way. "He was such an impressive man and such a powerful orator, so it was very brave of her to confront him. He knew so much about the word of God and he had a lot of people following him all the time, so seeing him walking into a village must have been quite awe-inspiring. And yet this woman wanted his attention so much that she overcame her fears and persevered with her request. I admire that."

The widow's offering

The widow in Mark 12:41–44 is a good example of how Jesus noticed and understood motivation. The poor woman humbly gave all that she had to live on, while the rich people proudly gave away but a token of their spare money, and expected God to bless them as a result. Jesus was sitting near the temple treasury, watching the people. "It's a lovely image of our Lord just sitting there quietly contemplating all that is going on around him," says Wendy. "The whole idea of him coming from heaven to be a man and living amongst us, doing all the everyday things of life, is quite wonderful. It makes him so real.

The little, ordinary things about Jesus' life are not mentioned in the Gospels, but he must have blown his nose and stubbed his toe, like all of us do. At Christmas I often think of him as a vulnerable baby in nappies, relying on his mother to breast-feed him. Later she would have spoon-fed him and she would have taught him to hold a cup.

"Someone who is interested in people and loves them will be someone who watches what they do. I suppose it can be seen as being nosey, but understanding a person's character and motivation is a key part of being an actor. By observing, we learn about someone in order to portray a more life-like character. Jesus was just casually noticing the ones with humble hearts, just as he does today. It's impossible for him to reach out and help those who feel that they need nothing from him."

A mum's-eye view

Unlike the Gospels of Matthew and Luke, Mark's Gospel does not record the birth of Jesus. As a mother, however, Wendy really relates to all the emotions that Mary, the mother of Jesus, must have experienced. Wendy thinks Mary must have kept very quiet about the impending birth of the Saviour, for fear that no one would believe her. "Fortunately for her, Joseph had had a dream telling him what was happening, so at least he was able to support her at this confusing time. I'm sure she only knew half the story, and was unaware of the fact that 33 years later her son would die in agony on a cross."

It's interesting to note that Joseph is not mentioned in the later parts of the Gospels, which suggests that he had died before Jesus started his ministry. This reinforces Wendy's image of Mary as a strong and courageous woman. She felt terribly distressed when her son was crucified, but somehow she did not try to fight against it, because she knew in her heart that it was meant to be. As Wendy says, "It must have been appalling to see her child suffer like that. In one of the other Gospels it says that he looked down from the cross and asked John to take care of his mother. That is so typical of Jesus. Maybe Mary looked up at him and thought, 'He's always thinking of other people – even when he's hanging on a cross!'"

Struggling

Peter was one of the most outspoken of Jesus' disciples. He was the one who had walked on the water and had said that he was willing to die for his master, and yet in Chapter 14 we find him denying Christ. Wendy has a great concern for those whose faith has drifted. What such people don't need is criticism; what they do need is help to understand that God still loves them. "God wants us back with him, no matter how far we have wandered away," says Wendy. "I know this from my own experience. Believe me, I was far away. I think it is very difficult to help someone who is struggling with his or her faith without coming across as Bible-bashing or pressurizing, so it's often better just to pray. Sometimes you just have to leave things in God's hands and trust him."

Wendy finds that "trust" is the key word in her Christian faith. "Just trust," she says. "You have given yourself to God, so now trust him. Of course, it's easy to forget to trust, and you can get tangled up in trying to solve this or that problem. You have to tell yourself, 'Shut up! Stop! Think for a moment. Trust God.' I find myself doing this constantly."

Even when we do fail, God is still there for us. Wendy has a friend who was once close to God but was pulled away from her faith by the stresses of life. She fell into an affair which almost destroyed her marriage and her relationship with her children, and desperately wished that she could turn back the clock. Too guilty and scared to approach God or her friends at church, she felt totally condemned and didn't know which way to turn. Wendy points out that "The woman may have moved away from God, but God hadn't moved away from her. The extraordinary thing is that God still loves her every bit as much as he did before, and he is just waiting for her to come back. He wouldn't force or cajole her, but he would woo her. The most important thing is not to feel condemned. We are surely all as bad as each other. We Christians really are in a tough battle – Satan makes it so. He puts all sorts of temptations in our path."

You can do it!

If there is one verse in Mark's Gospel that stands out for Wendy and encourages her on a rainy day, it's the one where Jesus says, "Everything is possible for the person who has faith" (Mark 9:23). "This verse helps to bolster up my faith when I'm feeling a little low," says Wendy. "It's the sort of verse that makes me tell myself, 'You can do it, Wendy!' We can't be living on a mountain-top all the time, and there are days when I feel lonely, anxious and concerned about the future, just like everyone else. The valleys of life are just as important as the mountains, and are often of much more use to us in terms of learning through experience. But this verse helps me to overcome my deepest fears and reminds me that there is always hope when I trust in God. There are some things that only he can understand. I am content to live my life to the best of my ability. Sometimes I see it as a 'dress rehearsal', and I know that one day God will say, 'The dress rehearsal is over, Wendy – now come and do the performance!'

"I used to be terrified of dying, wondering where I was going and what it would be like. I still have a fear of pain. I'm not a terribly brave person, but I do trust that God will see me through any of that. As far as heaven is concerned, I'm really looking forward to seeing Jack and all my Christian friends who have passed on. Of course, I am so very excited about meeting Jesus. That's going to be amazing, isn't it?"

What is it that fundamentally helps Wendy to hang on to her faith through both the good times and the bad? She says, "I truly believe there is a God, and that Jesus was God's Son, sent to us to show us the way back to God. Jesus' death on the cross was like building a bridge between us and God, making it possible for us to reach God. I remember my experiences of God, I rely on other Christians, I get in touch with my own feelings in relationship to God, and I pray, but ultimately I read his word, the scriptures. Here I find answers, understanding, comfort, compassion, a lot to be challenged by and a never-ending resource for my life today. Mark's Gospel and the life of Jesus are very much a central and crucial part of that."

The word "gospel" means "good news". It's obvious that for Wendy, it's wonderfully good news that there is a loving God who is with you right through your life on earth, caring, guiding and helping. "Even at the end of your life," she says, "it isn't the end – it's really just the beginning." For Wendy this is the best news of all.

Wendy's prayer

Father God, thank you for loving us, and through your love strengthening us, so that we can go forward in the full confidence of knowing that we are your children, and that nothing can ever separate us from your love. Amen.

Further help

This book contains two stories. One is the story of Wendy Craig and the other is the story of Jesus Christ taken from Mark's Gospel in the Bible. There are millions of people around the world who, like Wendy, say that discovering Jesus has changed their lives completely. If you would like to find out more, here are some suggestions:

- Talk to someone you know who is a practising Christian.
- Find a Bible and read some more (we have used the *Good News Bible* version of Mark's Gospel).
- Find a local church where people are willing to explain more about the Christian faith.

- Read some other books about people finding Jesus, such as *The Cross and the Switchblade* by David Wilkerson, *The Joni Story* by Joni Eareckson Tada and *Under the Influence* by Julia Fisher (all published by HarperCollins*Religious*).

Useful addresses

- Christian Enquiry Agency, Inter-church House, 35 Lower Marsh, London SE1 7RL. Tel: 0171 620 4444.
- Bible Society, Stonehill Green, Westlea, Swindon, Wilts. SN5 7DG. Tel: 01793 418100.
- Christians in Entertainment, PO Box 3019, South Croydon, Surrey CR2 7PJ.

THE STORY OF
JESUS
CHRIST

AS TOLD IN THE
GOSPEL OF MARK

Introduction

The Gospel according to Mark begins with the statement that it is "the Good News about Jesus Christ, the Son of God". Jesus is pictured as a man of action and authority. His authority is seen in his teaching, in his power over demons, and in forgiving people's sins. Jesus speaks of himself as the Son of Man, who came to give his life to set people free from sin.

Mark presents the story of Jesus in a straightforward, vigorous way, with emphasis on what Jesus did, rather than on his words and teachings. After a brief prologue about John the Baptist and the baptism and temptation of Jesus, the writer immediately takes up Jesus' ministry of healing and teaching. As time goes on, the followers of Jesus come to understand him better, but Jesus' opponents become more hostile. The closing chapters report the events of Jesus' last week of earthly life, especially his crucifixion and resurrection.

The two endings to the Gospel, which are enclosed in brackets, are generally regarded as written by someone other than the author of *Mark*.

Outline of Contents

The Preaching of John the Baptist

1 This is the Good News about Jesus Christ, the Son of God. [a] 2 It began as the prophet Isaiah had written: "God said, 'I will send my messenger ahead of you to clear the way for you.'

3 Someone is shouting in the desert,

'Get the road ready for the Lord;

make a straight path for him to travel!' "

4 So John appeared in the desert, baptizing and preaching. [b] "Turn away from your sins and be baptized," he told the people, "and God will forgive your sins." 5 Many people from the province of Judea and the city of Jerusalem went out to hear John. They confessed their sins, and he baptized them in the River Jordan.

a 1.1 *Some manuscripts do not have* the Son of God.
b 1.4 John appeared in the desert, baptizing and preaching; *some manuscripts have* John the Baptist appeared in the desert, preaching.

[6] John wore clothes made of camel's hair, with a leather belt round his waist, and his food was locusts and wild honey. [7] He announced to the people, "The man who will come after me is much greater than I am. I am not good enough even to bend down and untie his sandals. [8] I baptize you with water, but he will baptize you with the Holy Spirit."

The Baptism and Temptation of Jesus

[9] Not long afterwards Jesus came from Nazareth in the province of Galilee, and was baptized by John in the Jordan. [10] As soon as Jesus came up out of the water, he saw heaven opening and the Spirit coming down on him like a dove. [11] And a voice came from heaven, "You are my own dear Son. I am pleased with you."

[12] At once the Spirit made him go into the desert, [13] where he stayed 40 days, being tempted by Satan. Wild animals were there also, but angels came and helped him.

Jesus Calls Four Fishermen

[14] After John had been put in prison, Jesus went to Galilee and preached the Good News from God. [15] "The right time has come," he said, "and the Kingdom of God is near! Turn away from your sins and believe the Good News!"

¹⁶ As Jesus walked along the shore of Lake Galilee, he saw two fishermen, Simon and his brother Andrew, catching fish with a net. ¹⁷ Jesus said to them, "Come with me, and I will teach you to catch people." ¹⁸ At once they left their nets and went with him.

¹⁹ He went a little farther on and saw two other brothers, James and John, the sons of Zebedee. They were in their boat getting their nets ready. ²⁰ As soon as Jesus saw them, he called them; they left their father Zebedee in the boat with the hired men and went with Jesus.

A Man with an Evil Spirit

²¹ Jesus and his disciples came to the town of Capernaum, and on the next Sabbath Jesus went to the synagogue and began to teach. ²² The people who heard him were amazed at the way he taught, for he wasn't like the teachers of the Law; instead, he taught with authority.

²³ Just then a man with an evil spirit in him came into the synagogue and screamed, ²⁴ "What do you want with us, Jesus of Nazareth? Are you here to destroy us? I know who you are – you are God's holy messenger!"

²⁵ Jesus ordered the spirit, "Be quiet, and come out of the man!"

²⁶ The evil spirit shook the man hard, gave a loud scream, and came out of him. ²⁷ The people were all so amazed that they started saying to one another, "What is

this? Is it some kind of new teaching? This man has authority to give orders to the evil spirits, and they obey him!"

[28] And so the news about Jesus spread quickly everywhere in the province of Galilee.

Jesus Heals Many People

[29] Jesus and his disciples, including James and John, left the synagogue and went straight to the home of Simon and Andrew. [30] Simon's mother-in-law was sick in bed with a fever, and as soon as Jesus arrived, he was told about her. [31] He went to her, took her by the hand, and helped her up. The fever left her, and she began to wait on them.

[32] After the sun had set and evening had come, people brought to Jesus all the sick and those who had demons. [33] All the people of the town gathered in front of the house. [34] Jesus healed many who were sick with all kinds of diseases and drove out many demons. He would not let the demons say anything, because they knew who he was.

Jesus Preaches in Galilee

[35] Very early the next morning, long before daylight, Jesus got up and left the house. He went out of the town to a lonely place, where he prayed. [36] But Simon and his companions went out searching for him, [37] and when they found him, they said, "Everyone is looking for you."

[38] But Jesus answered, "We must go on to the other

villages round here. I have to preach in them also, because that is why I came."

[39] So he travelled all over Galilee, preaching in the synagogues and driving out demons.

Jesus Heals a Man

[40] A man suffering from a dreaded skin disease came to Jesus, knelt down, and begged him for help. "If you want to," he said, "you can make me clean."[a]

[41] Jesus was filled with pity,[b] and stretched out his hand and touched him. "I do want to," he answered. "Be clean!" [42] At once the disease left the man, and he was clean. [43] Then Jesus spoke sternly to him and sent him away at once, [44] after saying to him, "Listen, don't tell anyone about this. But go straight to the priest and let him examine you; then in order to prove to everyone that you are cured, offer the sacrifice that Moses ordered."

[45] But the man went away and began to spread the news everywhere. Indeed, he talked so much that Jesus could not go into a town publicly. Instead, he stayed out in lonely places, and people came to him from everywhere.

a. 1.40 MAKE ME CLEAN: *This disease was considered to make a person ritually unclean.*
b. 1.41 pity; *some manuscripts have* anger.

Jesus Heals a Paralysed Man

2 A few days later Jesus went back to Capernaum, and the news spread that he was at home. [2] So many people came together that there was no room left, not even out in front of the door. Jesus was preaching the message to them [3] when four men arrived, carrying a paralysed man to Jesus. [4] Because of the crowd, however, they could not get the man to him. So they made a hole in the roof right above the place where Jesus was. When they had made an opening, they let the man down, lying on his mat. [5] Seeing how much faith they had, Jesus said to the paralysed man, "My son, your sins are forgiven."

[6] Some teachers of the Law who were sitting there thought to themselves, [7] "How does he dare to talk like this? This is blasphemy! God is the only one who can forgive sins!"

[8] At once Jesus knew what they were thinking, so he said to them, "Why do you think such things? [9] Is it easier to say to this paralysed man, 'Your sins are forgiven', or to say, 'Get up, pick up your mat, and walk'? [10] I will prove to you, then, that the Son of Man has authority on earth to forgive sins." So he said to the paralysed man, [11] "I tell you, get up, pick up your mat, and go home!"

[12] While they all watched, the man got up, picked up his mat, and hurried away. They were all completely

amazed and praised God, saying, "We have never seen anything like this!"

Jesus Calls Levi

[13] Jesus went back again to the shore of Lake Galilee. A crowd came to him, and he started teaching them. [14] As he walked along, he saw a tax collector, Levi son of Alphaeus, sitting in his office. Jesus said to him, "Follow me." Levi got up and followed him.

[15] Later on Jesus was having a meal in Levi's house.[a] A large number of tax collectors and other outcasts were following Jesus, and many of them joined him and his disciples at the table. [16] Some teachers of the Law, who were Pharisees, saw that Jesus was eating with these outcasts and tax collectors, so they asked his disciples, "Why does he eat with such people?"

[17] Jesus heard them and answered, "People who are well do not need a doctor, but only those who are sick. I have not come to call respectable people, but outcasts."

The Question about Fasting

[18] On one occasion the followers of John the Baptist and the Pharisees were fasting. Some people came to Jesus and asked him, "Why is it that the disciples of John

a. 2.15 in Levi's house; *or* in his (*that is,* Jesus') house.

the Baptist and the disciples of the Pharisees fast, but yours do not?"

19 Jesus answered, "Do you expect the guests at a wedding party to go without food? Of course not! As long as the bridegroom is with them, they will not do that. 20 But the day will come when the bridegroom will be taken away from them, and then they will fast.

21 "No one uses a piece of new cloth to patch up an old coat, because the new patch will shrink and tear off some of the old cloth, making an even bigger hole. 22 Nor does anyone pour new wine into used wineskins, because the wine will burst the skins, and both the wine and the skins will be ruined. Instead, new wine must be poured into fresh wineskins."

The Question about the Sabbath

23 Jesus was walking through some cornfields on the Sabbath. As his disciples walked along with him, they began to pick the ears of corn. 24 So the Pharisees said to Jesus, "Look, it is against our Law for your disciples to do that on the Sabbath!"

25 Jesus answered, "Have you never read what David did that time when he needed something to eat? He and his men were hungry, 26 so he went into the house of God and ate the bread offered to God. This happened when Abiathar was the High Priest. According to our Law only

the priests may eat this bread – but David ate it and even gave it to his men."

²⁷ And Jesus concluded, "The Sabbath was made for the good of human beings; they were not made for the Sabbath. ²⁸ So the Son of Man is Lord even of the Sabbath."

The Man with a Paralysed Hand

3 Then Jesus went back to the synagogue, where there was a man who had a paralysed hand. ² Some people were there who wanted to accuse Jesus of doing wrong; so they watched him closely to see whether he would heal the man on the Sabbath. ³ Jesus said to the man, "Come up here to the front." ⁴ Then he asked the people, "What does our Law allow us to do on the Sabbath? To help or to harm? To save someone's life or to destroy it?"

But they did not say a thing. ⁵ Jesus was angry as he looked round at them, but at the same time he felt sorry for them, because they were so stubborn and wrong. Then he said to the man, "Stretch out your hand." He stretched it out, and it became well again. ⁶ So the Pharisees left the synagogue and met at once with some members of Herod's party, and they made plans to kill Jesus.

A Crowd by the Lake

⁷ Jesus and his disciples went away to Lake Galilee, and a large crowd followed him. They had come from Galilee, from Judea, ⁸ from Jerusalem, from the territory of Idumea, from the territory on the east side of the Jordan, and from the region round the cities of Tyre and Sidon. All these people came to Jesus because they had heard of the things he was doing. ⁹ The crowd was so large that Jesus told his disciples to get a boat ready for him, so that the people would not crush him. ¹⁰ He had healed many people, and all those who were ill kept pushing their way to him in order to touch him. ¹¹ And whenever the people who had evil spirits in them saw him, they would fall down before him and scream, "You are the Son of God!"

¹² Jesus sternly ordered the evil spirits not to tell anyone who he was.

Jesus Chooses the Twelve Apostles

¹³ Then Jesus went up a hill and called to himself the men he wanted. They came to him, ¹⁴ and he chose twelve, whom he named apostles. "I have chosen you to be with me," he told them. "I will also send you out to preach, ¹⁵ and you will have authority to drive out demons."

¹⁶ These are the twelve he chose: Simon (Jesus gave

him the name Peter); [17] James and his brother John, the sons of Zebedee (Jesus gave them the name Boanerges, which means "Men of Thunder"); [18] Andrew, Philip, Bartholomew, Matthew, Thomas, James son of Alphaeus, Thaddaeus, Simon the Patriot, [19] and Judas Iscariot, who betrayed Jesus.

Jesus and Beelzebul

[20] Then Jesus went home. Again such a large crowd gathered that Jesus and his disciples had no time to eat. [21] When his family heard about it, they set out to take charge of him, because people were saying, "He's gone mad!"

[22] Some teachers of the Law who had come from Jerusalem were saying, "He has Beelzebul in him! It is the chief of the demons who gives him the power to drive them out."

[23] So Jesus called them to him and spoke to them in parables: "How can Satan drive out Satan? [24] If a country divides itself into groups which fight each other, that country will fall apart. [25] If a family divides itself into groups which fight each other, that family will fall apart. [26] So if Satan's kingdom divides into groups, it cannot last, but will fall apart and come to an end.

[27] "No one can break into a strong man's house and take away his belongings unless he first ties up the strong man; then he can plunder his house.

[28] "I assure you that people can be forgiven all their sins and all the evil things they may say. [a] [29] But whoever says evil things against the Holy Spirit will never be forgiven, because he has committed an eternal sin." [30] (Jesus said this because some people were saying, "He has an evil spirit in him.")

Jesus' Mother and Brothers

[31] Then Jesus' mother and brothers arrived. They stood outside the house and sent in a message, asking for him. [32] A crowd was sitting round Jesus, and they said to him, "Look, your mother and your brothers and sisters are outside, and they want you."

[33] Jesus answered, "Who is my mother? Who are my brothers?" [34] He looked at the people sitting round him and said, "Look! Here are my mother and my brothers! [35] Whoever does what God wants him to do is my brother, my sister, my mother."

The Parable of the Sower

4 Again Jesus began to teach beside Lake Galilee. The crowd that gathered round him was so large that he got into a boat and sat in it. The boat was out in the

---

a 3.28 *evil things they may say; or* evil things they may say against God.

water, and the crowd stood on the shore at the water's edge. ² He used parables to teach them many things, saying to them:

³ "Listen! Once there was a man who went out to sow corn. ⁴ As he scattered the seed in the field, some of it fell along the path, and the birds came and ate it up. ⁵ Some of it fell on rocky ground, where there was little soil. The seeds soon sprouted, because the soil wasn't deep. ⁶ Then, when the sun came up, it burnt the young plants; and because the roots had not grown deep enough, the plants soon dried up. ⁷ Some of the seed fell among thorn bushes, which grew up and choked the plants, and they didn't produce any corn. ⁸ But some seeds fell in good soil, and the plants sprouted, grew, and produced corn: some had thirty grains, others sixty, and others a hundred."

⁹ And Jesus concluded, "Listen, then, if you have ears!"

The Purpose of the Parables

¹⁰ When Jesus was alone, some of those who had heard him came to him with the twelve disciples and asked him to explain the parables. ¹¹ "You have been given the secret of the Kingdom of God," Jesus answered. "But the others, who are on the outside, hear all things by means of parables, ¹² so that,

'They may look and look,
    yet not see;

they may listen and listen,
     yet not understand.
For if they did, they would turn to God,
     and he would forgive them.' "

Jesus Explains the Parable of the Sower

¹³ Then Jesus asked them, "Don't you understand this parable? How, then, will you ever understand any parable? ¹⁴ The sower sows God's message. ¹⁵ Some people are like the seeds that fall along the path; as soon as they hear the message, Satan comes and takes it away. ¹⁶ Other people are like the seeds that fall on rocky ground. As soon as they hear the message, they receive it gladly. ¹⁷ But it does not sink deep into them, and they don't last long. So when trouble or persecution comes because of the message, they give up at once. ¹⁸ Other people are like the seeds sown among the thorn bushes. These are the ones who hear the message, ¹⁹ but the worries about this life, the love for riches, and all other kinds of desires crowd in and choke the message, and they don't bear fruit. ²⁰ But other people are like the seeds sown in good soil. They hear the message, accept it, and bear fruit: some thirty, some sixty, and some a hundred."

A Lamp under a Bowl

²¹ Jesus continued, "Does anyone ever bring in a lamp and put it under a bowl or under the bed? Doesn't he put

it on the lampstand? ²² Whatever is hidden away will be brought out into the open, and whatever is covered up will be uncovered. ²³ Listen, then, if you have ears!"

²⁴ He also said to them, "Pay attention to what you hear! The same rules you use to judge others will be used by God to judge you – but with even greater severity. ²⁵ Those who have something will be given more, and those who have nothing will have taken away from them even the little they have."

The Parable of the Growing Seed

²⁶ Jesus went on to say, "The Kingdom of God is like this. A man scatters seed in his field.²⁷ He sleeps at night, is up and about during the day, and all the while the seeds are sprouting and growing. Yet he does not know how it happens. ²⁸ The soil itself makes the plants grow and bear fruit; first the tender stalk appears, then the ear, and finally the ear full of corn. ²⁹ When the corn is ripe, the man starts cutting it with his sickle, because harvest time has come.

The Parable of the Mustard Seed

³⁰ "What shall we say the Kingdom of God is like?" asked Jesus. "What parable shall we use to explain it? ³¹ It is like this. A man takes a mustard seed, the smallest seed in the world, and plants it in the ground. ³² After a while

it grows up and becomes the biggest of all plants. It puts out such large branches that the birds come and make their nests in its shade."

[33] Jesus preached his message to the people, using many other parables like these; he told them as much as they could understand. [34] He would not speak to them without using parables, but when he was alone with his disciples, he would explain everything to them.

Jesus Calms a Storm

[35] On the evening of that same day Jesus said to his disciples, "Let us go across to the other side of the lake." [36] So they left the crowd; the disciples got into the boat in which Jesus was already sitting, and they took him with them. Other boats were there too. [37] Suddenly a strong wind blew up, and the waves began to spill over into the boat, so that it was about to fill with water. [38] Jesus was in the back of the boat, sleeping with his head on a pillow. The disciples woke him up and said, "Teacher, don't you care that we are about to die?"

[39] Jesus stood up and commanded the wind, "Be quiet!" and he said to the waves, "Be still!" The wind died down, and there was a great calm. [40] Then Jesus said to his disciples, "Why are you frightened? Have you still no faith?"

[41] But they were terribly afraid and said to one another, "Who is this man? Even the wind and the waves obey him!"

Jesus Heals a Man with Evil Spirits

5 Jesus and his disciples arrived on the other side of Lake Galilee, in the territory of Gerasa. ² As soon as Jesus got out of the boat, he was met by a man who came out of the burial caves there. This man had an evil spirit in him ³ and lived among the tombs. Nobody could keep him chained up any more; ⁴ many times his feet and hands had been chained, but every time he broke the chains and smashed the irons on his feet. He was too strong for anyone to control him. ⁵ Day and night he wandered among the tombs and through the hills, screaming and cutting himself with stones.

⁶ He was some distance away when he saw Jesus; so he ran, fell on his knees before him, ⁷ and screamed in a loud voice, "Jesus, Son of the Most High God! What do you want with me? For God's sake, I beg you, don't punish me!" ⁸ (He said this because Jesus was saying, "Evil spirit, come out of this man!")

⁹ So Jesus asked him, "What is your name?"

The man answered, "My name is 'Mob' – there are so many of us!" ¹⁰ And he kept begging Jesus not to send the evil spirits out of that region.

¹¹ There was a large herd of pigs near by, feeding on a hillside. ¹² So the spirits begged Jesus, "Send us to the pigs, and let us go into them." ¹³ He let them go, and the evil spirits went out of the man and entered the pigs.

The whole herd – about 2,000 pigs in all – rushed down the side of the cliff into the lake and was drowned.

[14] The men who had been taking care of the pigs ran away and spread the news in the town and among the farms. People went out to see what had happened, [15] and when they came to Jesus, they saw the man who used to have the mob of demons in him. He was sitting there, clothed and in his right mind; and they were all afraid. [16] Those who had seen it told the people what had happened to the man with the demons, and about the pigs.

[17] So they asked Jesus to leave their territory.

[18] As Jesus was getting into the boat, the man who had had the demons begged him, "Let me go with you!"

[19] But Jesus would not let him. Instead, he told him, "Go back home to your family and tell them how much the Lord has done for you and how kind he has been to you."

[20] So the man left and went all through the Ten Towns, telling what Jesus had done for him. And all who heard it were amazed.

Jairus' Daughter and the Woman who Touched Jesus' Cloak

[21] Jesus went back across to the other side of the lake. There at the lakeside a large crowd gathered round him.

²² Jairus, an official of the local synagogue, arrived, and when he saw Jesus, he threw himself down at his feet ²³ and begged him earnestly, "My little daughter is very ill. Please come and place your hands on her, so that she will get well and live!"

²⁴ Then Jesus started off with him. So many people were going along with Jesus that they were crowding him from every side.

²⁵ There was a woman who had suffered terribly from severe bleeding for twelve years, ²⁶ even though she had been treated by many doctors. She had spent all her money, but instead of getting better she got worse all the time. ²⁷ She had heard about Jesus, so she came in the crowd behind him, ²⁸ saying to herself, "If I just touch his clothes, I will get well."

²⁹ She touched his cloak, and her bleeding stopped at once; and she had the feeling inside herself that she was healed of her trouble. ³⁰ At once Jesus knew that power had gone out of him, so he turned round in the crowd and asked, "Who touched my clothes?"

³¹ His disciples answered, "You see how the people are crowding you; why do you ask who touched you?"

³² But Jesus kept looking round to see who had done it. ³³ The woman realized what had happened to her, so she came, trembling with fear, knelt at his feet, and told him the whole truth. ³⁴ Jesus said to her, "My daughter,

your faith has made you well. Go in peace, and be healed of your trouble."

³⁵ While Jesus was saying this, some messengers came from Jairus' house and told him, "Your daughter has died. Why bother the Teacher any longer?"

³⁶ Jesus paid no attention to ᵃ what they said, but told him, "Don't be afraid, only believe." ³⁷ Then he did not let anyone else go on with him except Peter and James and his brother John. ³⁸ They arrived at Jairus' house, where Jesus saw the confusion and heard all the loud crying and wailing. ³⁹ He went in and said to them, "Why all this confusion? Why are you crying? The child is not dead – she is only sleeping!"

⁴⁰ They laughed at him, so he put them all out, took the child's father and mother and his three disciples, and went into the room where the child was lying. ⁴¹ He took her by the hand and said to her, "*Talitha, koum,*" which means, "Little girl, I tell you to get up!"

⁴² She got up at once and started walking around. (She was twelve years old.) When this happened, they were completely amazed. ⁴³ But Jesus gave them strict orders not to tell anyone, and he said, "Give her something to eat."

a 5.36 paid no attention to; *or* overheard.

Jesus is Rejected at Nazareth

6 Jesus left that place and went back to his home town, followed by his disciples. ² On the Sabbath he began to teach in the synagogue. Many people were there; and when they heard him, they were all amazed. "Where did he get all this?" they asked. "What wisdom is this that has been given him? How does he perform miracles? ³ Isn't he the carpenter, the son of Mary, and the brother of James, Joseph, Judas, and Simon? Aren't his sisters living here?" And so they rejected him.

⁴ Jesus said to them, "Prophets are respected everywhere except in their own home town and by their relatives and their family."

⁵ He was not able to perform any miracles there, except that he placed his hands on a few sick people and healed them. ⁶ He was greatly surprised, because the people did not have faith.

Jesus Sends out the Twelve Disciples

Then Jesus went to the villages round there, teaching the people. ⁷ He called the twelve disciples together and sent them out two by two. He gave them authority over the evil spirits ⁸ and ordered them, "Don't take anything with you on your journey except a stick – no bread, no beggar's bag, no money in your pockets. ⁹ Wear sandals, but don't carry an extra shirt." ¹⁰ He also said, "Wherever you are welcomed, stay in the same house until you leave that place. [11] If you come to a town where people do not welcome you or will not listen to you, leave it and shake the dust off your feet. That will be a warning to them!"

[12] So they went out and preached that people should turn away from their sins. [13] They drove out many demons, and rubbed olive oil on many sick people and healed them.

The Death of John the Baptist

[14] Now King Herod [a] heard about all this, because Jesus' reputation had spread everywhere. Some people were saying, "John the Baptist has come back to life! That is why he has this power to perform miracles."

[15] Others, however, said, "He is Elijah."

Others said, "He is a prophet, like one of the prophets of long ago."

[16] When Herod heard it, he said, "He is John the Baptist! I had his head cut off, but he has come back to life!" [17] Herod himself had ordered John's arrest, and he had him chained and put in prison. Herod did this because of Herodias, whom he had married, even though she was the wife of his brother Philip. [18] John the Baptist kept telling Herod, "It isn't right for you to be married to your brother's wife!"

a 6.14 KING HEROD: *Herod Antipas, ruler of Galilee.*

¹⁹ So Herodias held a grudge against John and wanted to kill him, but she could not because of Herod. ²⁰ Herod was afraid of John because he knew that John was a good and holy man, and so he kept him safe. He liked to listen to him, even though he became greatly disturbed every time he heard him.

²¹ Finally Herodias got her chance. It was on Herod's birthday, when he gave a feast for all the chief government officials, the military commanders, and the leading citizens of Galilee. ²² The daughter of Herodias ᵃ came in and danced, and pleased Herod and his guests. So the king said to the girl, "What would you like to have? I will give you anything you want." ²³ With many vows he said to her, "I swear that I will give you anything you ask for, even as much as half my kingdom!"

²⁴ So the girl went out and asked her mother, "What shall I ask for?"

"The head of John the Baptist," she answered.

²⁵ The girl hurried back at once to the king and demanded, "I want you to give me here and now the head of John the Baptist on a dish!"

²⁶ This made the king very sad, but he could not refuse her because of the vows he had made in front of all his

---

a 6.22 The daughter of Herodias; *some manuscripts have* His daughter Herodias.

guests. ²⁷ So he sent off a guard at once with orders to bring John's head. The guard left, went to the prison, and cut John's head off; ²⁸ then he brought it on a dish and gave it to the girl, who gave it to her mother. ²⁹ When John's disciples heard about this, they came and took away his body, and buried it.

Jesus Feeds a Great Crowd

³⁰ The apostles returned and met with Jesus, and told him all they had done and taught. ³¹ There were so many people coming and going that Jesus and his disciples didn't even have time to eat. So he said to them, "Let us go off by ourselves to some place where we will be alone and you can rest for a while." ³² So they started out in a boat by themselves for a lonely place.

³³ Many people, however, saw them leave and knew at once who they were; so they went from all the towns and ran ahead by land and arrived at the place ahead of Jesus and his disciples. ³⁴ When Jesus got out of the boat, he saw this large crowd, and his heart was filled with pity for them, because they were like sheep without a shepherd. So he began to teach them many things. ³⁵ When it was getting late, his disciples came to him and said, "It is already very late, and this is a lonely place. ³⁶ Send the people away, and let them go to the nearby farms and villages in order to buy themselves something to eat."

[37] "You yourselves give them something to eat," Jesus answered.

They asked, "Do you want us to go and spend two hundred silver coins [a] on bread in order to feed them?"

[38] So Jesus asked them, "How much bread have you got? Go and see."

When they found out, they told him, "Five loaves and also two fish."

[39] Jesus then told his disciples to make all the people divide into groups and sit down on the green grass. [40] So the people sat down in rows, in groups of a hundred and groups of fifty. [41] Then Jesus took the five loaves and the two fish, looked up to heaven, and gave thanks to God. He broke the loaves and gave them to his disciples to distribute to the people. He also divided the two fish among them all. [42] Everyone ate and had enough. [43] Then the disciples took up twelve baskets full of what was left of the bread and the fish. [44] The number of men who were fed was 5,000.

Jesus Walks on the Water

[45] At once Jesus made his disciples get into the boat and go ahead of him to Bethsaida, on the other side of

a 6.37 SILVER COINS: *A silver coin was the daily wage of a rural worker (see Mt 20.2).*

the lake, while he sent the crowd away. ⁴⁶ After saying goodbye to the people he went away to a hill to pray. ⁴⁷ When evening came, the boat was in the middle of the lake, while Jesus was alone on land. ⁴⁸ He saw that his disciples were straining at the oars, because they were rowing against the wind; so some time between three and six o'clock in the morning he came to them, walking on the water. He was going to pass them by, ᵃ ⁴⁹ but they saw him walking on the water. "It's a ghost!" they thought, and screamed. ⁵⁰ They were all terrified when they saw him.

Jesus spoke to them at once, "Courage!" he said. "It is I. Don't be afraid!" ⁵¹ Then he got into the boat with them, and the wind died down. The disciples were completely amazed, ⁵² because they had not understood the real meaning of the feeding of the 5,000; their minds could not grasp it.

Jesus Heals the Sick in Gennesaret

⁵³ They crossed the lake and came to land at Gennesaret, where they tied up the boat. ⁵⁴ As they left the boat, people recognized Jesus at once. ⁵⁵ So they ran throughout the whole region; and wherever they heard he was, they brought to him sick people lying on their mats. ⁵⁶ And everywhere Jesus went, to villages, towns, or farms,

a 6.48 pass them by; *or* join them.

people would take those who were ill to the market places and beg him to let them at least touch the edge of his cloak; and all who touched it were made well.

The Teaching of the Ancestors

7 Some Pharisees and teachers of the Law who had come from Jerusalem gathered round Jesus. ² They noticed that some of his disciples were eating their food with hands that were ritually unclean – that is, they had not washed them in the way the Pharisees said people should.

³ (For the Pharisees, as well as the rest of the Jews, follow the teaching they received from their ancestors: they do not eat unless they wash their hands in the proper way; ⁴ nor do they eat anything that comes from the market unless they wash it first. ᵃ And they follow many other rules which they have received, such as the proper way to wash cups, pots, copper bowls, and beds. ᵇ)

⁵ So the Pharisees and the teachers of the Law asked Jesus, "Why is it that your disciples do not follow the teaching handed down by our ancestors, but instead eat with ritually unclean hands?"

a 7.4 anything that comes from the market unless they wash it first; *or* anything after they come from the market unless they wash themselves first.

b 7.4 *Some manuscripts do not have* and beds.

[6] Jesus answered them, "How right Isaiah was when he prophesied about you! You are hypocrites, just as he wrote:

'These people, says God, honour me with their words,
  but their heart is really far away from me.
[7] It is no use for them to worship me,
  because they teach human rules
  as though they were God's laws!'

[8] "You put aside God's command and obey human teachings."

[9] And Jesus continued, "You have a clever way of rejecting God's law in order to uphold your own teaching. [10] For Moses commanded, 'Respect your father and your mother,' and, 'Whoever curses his father or his mother is to be put to death.' [11] But you teach that if a person has something he could use to help his father or mother, but says, 'This is Corban' (which means, it belongs to God), [12] he is excused from helping his father or mother. [13] In this way the teaching you pass on to others cancels out the word of God. And there are many other things like this that you do."

The Things that Make a Person Unclean

[14] Then Jesus called the crowd to him once more and said to them, "Listen to me, all of you, and understand. [15] There is nothing that goes into a person from the

outside which can make him ritually unclean. Rather, it is what comes out of a person that makes him unclean." [a]

¹⁷ When he left the crowd and went into the house, his disciples asked him to explain this saying. ¹⁸ "You are no more intelligent than the others," Jesus said to them. "Don't you understand? Nothing that goes into a person from the outside can really make him unclean, ¹⁹ because it does not go into his heart but into his stomach and then goes on out of the body." (In saying this, Jesus declared that all foods are fit to be eaten.)

²⁰ And he went on to say, "It is what comes out of a person that makes him unclean. ²¹ For from the inside, from a person's heart, come the evil ideas which lead him to do immoral things, to rob, kill, ²² commit adultery, be greedy, and do all sorts of evil things; deceit, indecency, jealousy, slander, pride, and folly – ²³ all these evil things come from inside a person and make him unclean."

A Woman's Faith

²⁴ Then Jesus left and went away to the territory near the city of Tyre. He went into a house and did not want anyone to know he was there, but he could not stay hidden. ²⁵ A woman, whose daughter had an evil spirit in

a 7.15 *Some manuscripts add verse 16:* Listen, then, if you have ears! *(see 4.23).*

her, heard about Jesus and came to him at once and fell at his feet. 26 The woman was a Gentile, born in the region of Phoenicia in Syria. She begged Jesus to drive the demon out of her daughter. 27 But Jesus answered, "Let us first feed the children. It isn't right to take the children's food and throw it to the dogs."

28 "Sir," she answered, "even the dogs under the table eat the children's leftovers!"

29 So Jesus said to her, "Because of that answer, go back home, where you will find that the demon has gone out of your daughter!"

30 She went home and found her child lying on the bed; the demon had indeed gone out of her.

Jesus Heals a Deaf-mute

31 Jesus then left the neighbourhood of Tyre and went on through Sidon to Lake Galilee, going by way of the territory of the Ten Towns. 32 Some people brought him a man who was deaf and could hardly speak, and they begged Jesus to place his hands on him. 33 So Jesus took him off alone, away from the crowd, put his fingers in the man's ears, spat, and touched the man's tongue. 34 Then Jesus looked up to heaven, gave a deep groan, and said to the man, "*Ephphatha*," which means, "Open up!"

35 At once the man was able to hear, his speech impediment was removed, and he began to talk without any

trouble. ³⁶ Then Jesus ordered the people not to speak of it to anyone; but the more he ordered them not to, the more they spoke. ³⁷ And all who heard were completely amazed. "How well he does everything!" they exclaimed. "He even causes the deaf to hear and the dumb to speak!"

Jesus Feeds Four Thousand People

8 Not long afterwards another large crowd came together. When the people had nothing left to eat, Jesus called the disciples to him and said, ² "I feel sorry for these people, because they have been with me for three days and now have nothing to eat. ³ If I send them home without feeding them, they will faint as they go, because some of them have come a long way."

⁴ His disciples asked him, "Where in this desert can anyone find enough food to feed all these people?"

⁵ How much bread have you got?" Jesus asked.

"Seven loaves," they answered.

⁶ He ordered the crowd to sit down on the ground. Then he took the seven loaves, gave thanks to God, broke them, and gave them to his disciples to distribute to the crowd; and the disciples did so. ⁷ They also had a few small fish. Jesus gave thanks for these and told the disciples to distribute them too. ⁸⁻⁹ Everybody ate and had enough – there were about 4,000 people. Then the disciples took up seven baskets full of pieces left over.

Jesus sent the people away [10] and at once got into a boat with his disciples and went to the district of Dalmanutha.

The Pharisees Ask for a Miracle

[11] Some Pharisees came to Jesus and started to argue with him. They wanted to trap him, so they asked him to perform a miracle to show that God approved of him. [12] But Jesus gave a deep groan and said, "Why do the people of this day ask for a miracle? No, I tell you! No such proof will be given to these people!"

[13] He left them, got back into the boat, and started across to the other side of the lake.

The Yeast of the Pharisees and of Herod

[14] The disciples had forgotten to bring enough bread and had only one loaf with them in the boat. [15] "Take care," Jesus warned them, "and be on your guard against the yeast of the Pharisees and the yeast of Herod."

[16] They started discussing among themselves: "He says this because we haven't any bread."

[17] Jesus knew what they were saying, so he asked them, "Why are you discussing about not having any bread? Don't you know or understand yet? Are your minds so dull? [18] You have eyes – can't you see? You have ears – can't you hear? Don't you remember [19] when I broke the five

loaves for the five thousand people? How many baskets full of leftover pieces did you take up?"

"Twelve," they answered.

[20] "And when I broke the seven loaves for the four thousand people," asked Jesus, "how many baskets full of leftover pieces did you take up?"

"Seven," they answered.

[21] "And you still don't understand?" he asked them.

Jesus Heals a Blind Man at Bethsaida

[22] They came to Bethsaida, where some people brought a blind man to Jesus and begged him to touch him. [23] Jesus took the blind man by the hand and led him out of the village. After spitting on the man's eyes, Jesus placed his hands on him and asked him, "Can you see anything?"

[24] The man looked up and said, "Yes, I can see people, but they look like trees walking about."

[25] Jesus again placed his hands on the man's eyes. This time the man looked intently, his eyesight returned, and he saw everything clearly. [26] Jesus then sent him home with the order, "Don't go back into the village."

Peter's Declaration about Jesus

[27] Then Jesus and his disciples went away to the villages near Caesarea Philippi. On the way he asked them,

"Tell me, who do people say I am?"

[28] Some say that you are John the Baptist," they answered; "others say that you are Elijah, while others say that you are one of the prophets."

[29] "What about you?" he asked them. "Who do you say I am?"

Peter answered, "You are the Messiah."

[30] Then Jesus ordered them, "Do not tell anyone about me."

Jesus Speaks about his Suffering and Death

[31] Then Jesus began to teach his disciples: "The Son of Man must suffer much and be rejected by the elders, the chief priests, and the teachers of the Law. He will be put to death, but three days later he will rise to life." [32] He made this very clear to them. So Peter took him aside and began to rebuke him. [33] But Jesus turned round, looked at his disciples, and rebuked Peter. "Get away from me, Satan," he said. "Your thoughts don't come from God but from human nature!"

[34] Then Jesus called the crowd and his disciples to him. "If anyone wants to come with me," he told them, "he must forget self, carry his cross, and follow me. [35] For whoever wants to save his own life will lose it; but whoever loses his life for me and for the gospel will save it.

³⁶ Do people gain anything if they win the whole world but lose their life? Of course not! ³⁷ There is nothing they can give to regain their life. ³⁸ If a person is ashamed of me and of my teaching in this godless and wicked day, then the Son of Man will be ashamed of him when he comes in the glory of his Father with the holy angels."

9 And he went on to say, "I tell you, there are some here who will not die until they have seen the Kingdom of God come with power."

The Transfiguration

² Six days later Jesus took with him Peter, James and John, and led them up a high mountain, where they were alone. As they looked on, a change came over Jesus, ³ and his clothes became shining white – whiter than anyone in the world could wash them. ⁴ Then the three disciples saw Elijah and Moses talking with Jesus. ⁵ Peter spoke up and said to Jesus, "Teacher, how good it is that we are here! We will make three tents, one for you, one for Moses, and one for Elijah." ⁶ He and the others were so frightened that he did not know what to say.

⁷ Then a cloud appeared and covered them with its shadow, and a voice came from the cloud, "This is my own dear Son – listen to him!" ⁸ They took a quick look round but did not see anyone else; only Jesus was with them.

[9] As they came down the mountain, Jesus ordered them, "Don't tell anyone what you have seen, until the Son of Man has risen from death."

[10] They obeyed his order, but among themselves they started discussing the matter, "What does this 'rising from death' mean?" [11] And they asked Jesus, "Why do the teachers of the Law say that Elijah has to come first?"

[12] His answer was, "Elijah is indeed coming first in order to get everything ready. Yet why do the Scriptures say that the Son of Man will suffer much and be rejected? [13]I tell you, however, that Elijah has already come and that people treated him just as they pleased, as the Scriptures say about him."

Jesus Heals a Boy with an Evil Spirit

[14] When they joined the rest of the disciples, they saw a large crowd round them and some teachers of the Law arguing with them. [15] When the people saw Jesus, they were greatly surprised, and ran to him and greeted him. [16] Jesus asked his disciples, "What are you arguing with them about?"

[17] A man in the crowd answered, "Teacher, I brought my son to you, because he has an evil spirit in him and cannot talk. [18] Whenever the spirit attacks him, it throws him to the ground, and he foams at the mouth, grits his

teeth, and becomes stiff all over. I asked your disciples to drive the spirit out, but they could not."

¹⁹ Jesus said to them, "How unbelieving you people are! How long must I stay with you? How long do I have to put up with you? Bring the boy to me!" ²⁰ They brought him to Jesus.

As soon as the spirit saw Jesus, it threw the boy into a fit, so that he fell on the ground and rolled round, foaming at the mouth. ²¹ "How long has he been like this?" Jesus asked the father.

"Ever since he was a child," he replied. ²² "Many times the evil spirit has tried to kill him by throwing him in the fire and into water. Have pity on us and help us, if you possibly can!"

²³ "Yes," said Jesus, "if you yourself can! Everything is possible for the person who has faith."

²⁴ The father at once cried out, "I do have faith, but not enough. Help me to have more!"

²⁵ Jesus noticed that the crowd was closing in on them, so he gave a command to the evil spirit. "Deaf and dumb spirit," he said, "I order you to come out of the boy and never go into him again!"

²⁶ The spirit screamed, threw the boy into a bad fit, and came out. The boy looked like a corpse, and everyone said, "He is dead!" ²⁷ But Jesus took the boy by the hand and helped him to rise, and he stood up.

²⁸ After Jesus had gone indoors, his disciples asked him privately, "Why couldn't we drive the spirit out?"

²⁹ "Only prayer can drive this kind out," answered Jesus; "nothing else can."

Jesus Speaks Again about his Death

³⁰ Jesus and his disciples left that place and went on through Galilee. Jesus did not want anyone to know where he was, ³¹ because he was teaching his disciples: "The Son of Man will be handed over to those who will kill him. Three days later, however, he will rise to life."

³² But they did not understand what this teaching meant, and they were afraid to ask him.

Who is the Greatest?

³³ They came to Capernaum, and after going indoors Jesus asked his disciples, "What were you arguing about on the road?"

³⁴ But they would not answer him, because on the road they had been arguing among themselves about who was the greatest. ³⁵ Jesus sat down, called the twelve disciples, and said to them, "Whoever wants to be first must place himself last of all and be the servant of all." ³⁶ Then he took a child and made him stand in front of them. He put his arms round him and said to them, ³⁷ "Whoever welcomes in my name one of these children, welcomes

me; and whoever welcomes me, welcomes not only me but also the one who sent me."

Whoever is not Against Us is For Us

[38] John said to him, "Teacher, we saw a man who was driving out demons in your name, and we told him to stop, because he doesn't belong to our group."

[39] "Do not try to stop him," Jesus told them, "because no one who performs a miracle in my name will be able soon afterwards to say evil things about me. [40] For whoever is not against us is for us. [41] I assure you that anyone who gives you a drink of water because you belong to me will certainly receive his reward.

Temptations to Sin

[42] "If anyone should cause one of these little ones to lose his faith in me, it would be better for that person to have a large millstone tied round his neck and be thrown into the sea. [43] So if your hand makes you lose your faith, cut it off! It is better for you to enter life without a hand than to keep both hands and go off to hell, to the fire that never goes out. [a] [45] And if your foot makes you lose your faith, cut it off! It is better for you to enter life without a foot

a 9.43 *Some manuscripts add verse 44:* There 'the worms that eat them never die, and the fire that burns them is never put out' *(see verse 48).*

than to keep both feet and be thrown into hell. [b] [47] And if your eye makes you lose your faith, take it out! It is better for you to enter the Kingdom of God with only one eye than to keep both eyes and be thrown into hell. [48] There 'the worms that eat them never die, and the fire that burns them is never put out.'

[49] "Everyone will be purified by fire as a sacrifice is purified by salt.

[50] "Salt is good; but if it loses its saltiness, how can you make it salty again?

"Have the salt of friendship among yourselves, and live in peace with one another."

Jesus Teaches about Divorce

10 Then Jesus left that place, went to the province of Judea, and crossed the River Jordan. Crowds came flocking to him again, and he taught them, as he always did.

[2] Some Pharisees came to him and tried to trap him. "Tell us," they asked, "does our Law allow a man to divorce his wife?"

[3] Jesus answered with a question, "What law did Moses give you?"

b 9.45 *Some manuscripts add verse 46:* There 'the worms that eat them never die, and the fire that burns them is never put out' *(see verse 48).*

[4] Their answer was, "Moses gave permission for a man to write a divorce notice and send his wife away."

[5] Jesus said to them, "Moses wrote this law for you because you are so hard to teach. [6] But in the beginning, at the time of creation, 'God made them male and female,' as the scripture says. [7] 'And for this reason a man will leave his father and mother and unite with his wife,[a] [8] and the two will become one.' So they are no longer two, but one. [9] No human being then must separate what God has joined together."

[10] When they went back into the house, the disciples asked Jesus about this matter. [11] He said to them, "A man who divorces his wife and marries another woman commits adultery against his wife. [12] In the same way, a woman who divorces her husband and marries another man commits adultery."

Jesus Blesses Little Children

[13] Some people brought children to Jesus for him to place his hands on them, but the disciples scolded the people. [14] When Jesus noticed this, he was angry and said to his disciples, "Let the children come to me, and do not stop them, because the Kingdom of God belongs to such

a 10.7 *Some manuscripts do not have* and unite with his wife.

as these. [15] I assure you that whoever does not receive the Kingdom of God like a child will never enter it." [16] Then he took the children in his arms, placed his hands on each of them, and blessed them.

The Rich Man

[17] As Jesus was starting on his way again, a man ran up, knelt before him, and asked him, "Good Teacher, what must I do to receive eternal life?"

[18] "Why do you call me good?" Jesus asked him. "No one is good except God alone. [19] You know the commandments: 'Do not commit murder; do not commit adultery; do not steal; do not accuse anyone falsely; do not cheat; respect your father and your mother.' "

[20] "Teacher," the man said, "ever since I was young, I have obeyed all these commandments."

[21] Jesus looked straight at him with love and said, "You need only one thing. Go and sell all you have and give the money to the poor, and you will have riches in heaven; then come and follow me." [22] When the man heard this, gloom spread over his face, and he went away sad, because he was very rich.

[23] Jesus looked round at his disciples and said to them, "How hard it will be for rich people to enter the Kingdom of God!"

[24] The disciples were shocked at these words, but Jesus

went on to say, "My children, how hard it is to enter the Kingdom of God! [25] It is much harder for a rich person to enter the Kingdom of God than for a camel to go through the eye of a needle."

[26] At this the disciples were completely amazed and asked one another, "Who, then, can be saved?"

[27] Jesus looked straight at them and answered, "This is impossible for human beings, but not for God; everything is possible for God."

[28] Then Peter spoke up, "Look, we have left everything and followed you."

[29] "Yes," Jesus said to them, "and I tell you that anyone who leaves home or brothers or sisters or mother or father or children or fields for me and for the gospel, [30] will receive much more in this present age. He will receive a hundred times more houses, brothers, sisters, mothers, children and fields – and persecutions as well; and in the age to come he will receive eternal life. [31] But many who now are first will be last, and many who now are last will be first."

Jesus Speaks a Third Time about his Death

[32] Jesus and his disciples were now on the road going up to Jerusalem. Jesus was going ahead of the disciples, who were filled with alarm; the people who followed behind were afraid. Once again Jesus took the twelve

disciples aside and spoke of the things that were going to happen to him. ³³ "Listen," he told them, "we are going up to Jerusalem where the Son of Man will be handed over to the chief priests and the teachers of the Law. They will condemn him to death and then hand him over to the Gentiles, ³⁴ who will mock him, spit on him, whip him, and kill him; but three days later he will rise to life."

The Request of James and John

³⁵ Then James and John, the sons of Zebedee, came to Jesus. "Teacher," they said, "there is something we want you to do for us."

³⁶ "What is it?" Jesus asked them.

³⁷ They answered, "When you sit on your throne in your glorious Kingdom, we want you to let us sit with you, one at your right and one at your left."

³⁸ Jesus said to them, "You don't know what you are asking for. Can you drink the cup of suffering that I must drink? Can you be baptized in the way I must be baptized?"

³⁹ "We can," they answered.

Jesus said to them, "You will indeed drink the cup I must drink and be baptized in the way I must be baptized. ⁴⁰ But I do not have the right to choose who will sit at my right and my left. It is God who will give these places to those for whom he has prepared them."

[41] When the other ten disciples heard about it, they became angry with James and John. [42] So Jesus called them all together to him and said, "You know that those who are considered rulers of the heathen have power over them, and the leaders have complete authority. [43] This, however, is not the way it is among you. If one of you wants to be great, he must be the servant of the rest; [44] and if one of you wants to be first, he must be the slave of all. [45] For even the Son of Man did not come to be served; he came to serve and to give his life to redeem many people."

Jesus Heals Blind Bartimaeus

[46] They came to Jericho, and as Jesus was leaving with his disciples and a large crowd, a blind beggar named Bartimaeus son of Timaeus was sitting by the road. [47] When he heard that it was Jesus of Nazareth, he began to shout, "Jesus! Son of David! Take pity on me!"

[48] Many of the people scolded him and told him to be quiet. But he shouted even more loudly, "Son of David, take pity on me!"

[49] Jesus stopped and said, "Call him."

So they called the blind man. "Cheer up!" they said. "Get up, he is calling you."

[50] He threw off his cloak, jumped up, and came to Jesus.

⁵¹ "What do you want me to do for you?" Jesus asked him.

"Teacher," the blind man answered, "I want to see again."

⁵² "Go," Jesus told him, "your faith has made you well."

At once he was able to see and followed Jesus on the road.

The Triumphant Entry into Jerusalem

11 As they approached Jerusalem, near the towns of Bethphage and Bethany, they came to the Mount of Olives. Jesus sent two of his disciples on ahead ² with these instructions: "Go to the village there ahead of you. As soon as you get there, you will find a colt tied up that has never been ridden. Untie it and bring it here. ³ And if someone asks you why you are doing that, tell him that the Master ᵃ needs it and will send it back at once."

⁴ So they went and found a colt out in the street, tied to the door of a house. As they were untying it, ⁵ some of the bystanders asked them, "What are you doing, untying that colt?"

⁶ They answered just as Jesus had told them, and the bystanders let them go. ⁷ They brought the colt to Jesus, threw their cloaks over the animal, and Jesus got on.

a 11.3 the Master; *or* its owner.

[8] Many people spread their cloaks on the road, while others cut branches in the fields and spread them on the road. [9] The people who were in front and those who followed behind began to shout, "Praise God! God bless him who comes in the name of the Lord! [10] God bless the coming kingdom of King David, our father! Praise God!"

[11] Jesus entered Jerusalem, went into the Temple, and looked round at everything. But since it was already late in the day, he went out to Bethany with the twelve disciples.

Jesus Curses the Fig Tree

[12] The next day, as they were coming back from Bethany, Jesus was hungry. [13] He saw in the distance a fig tree covered with leaves, so he went to see if he could find any figs on it. But when he came to it, he found only leaves, because it was not the right time for figs. [14] Jesus said to the fig tree, "No one shall ever eat figs from you again!"

And his disciples heard him.

Jesus Goes to the Temple

[15] When they arrived in Jerusalem, Jesus went to the Temple and began to drive out all those who were buying and selling. He overturned the tables of the money-changers and the stools of those who sold pigeons, [16] and

he would not let anyone carry anything through the temple courtyards. [17] He then taught the people: "It is written in the Scriptures that God said, 'My Temple will be called a house of prayer for the people of all nations.' But you have turned it into a hideout for thieves!"

[18] The chief priests and the teachers of the Law heard of this, so they began looking for some way to kill Jesus. They were afraid of him, because the whole crowd was amazed at his teaching.

[19] When evening came, Jesus and his disciples left the city.

The Lesson from the Fig Tree

[20] Early next morning, as they walked along the road, they saw the fig tree. It was dead all the way down to its roots. [21] Peter remembered what had happened and said to Jesus, "Look, Teacher, the fig tree you cursed has died!"

[22] Jesus answered them, "Have faith in God. [23] I assure you that whoever tells this hill to get up and throw itself in the sea and does not doubt in his heart, but believes that what he says will happen, it will be done for him. [24] For this reason I tell you: when you pray and ask for something, believe that you have received it, and you will be given whatever you ask for. [25] And when you stand and pray, forgive anything you may have against anyone, so

that your Father in heaven will forgive the wrongs you have done." [a]

The Question about Jesus' Authority

[27] They arrived once again in Jerusalem. As Jesus was walking in the Temple, the chief priests, the teachers of the Law, and the elders came to him [28] and asked him, "What right have you to do these things? Who gave you this right?"

[29] Jesus answered them, "I will ask you just one question, and if you give me an answer, I will tell you what right I have to do these things. [30] Tell me, where did John's right to baptize come from: was it from God or from human beings?"

[31] They started to argue among themselves: "What shall we say? If we answer, 'From God,' he will say, 'Why, then, did you not believe John?' [32] But if we say, 'From human beings …'" (They were afraid of the people, because everyone was convinced that John had been a prophet.) [33] So their answer to Jesus, was, "We don't know."

Jesus said to them, "Neither will I tell you, then, by what right I do these things."

a 11.25 *Some manuscripts add verse 26:* If you do not forgive others, your Father in heaven will not forgive the wrongs you have done *(see Mt 6.15).*

The Parable of the Tenants in the Vineyard

12 Then Jesus spoke to them in parables: "Once there was a man who planted a vineyard, put a fence round it, dug a hole for the winepress, and built a watchtower. Then he let out the vineyard to tenants and left home on a journey. ² When the time came to gather the grapes, he sent a slave to the tenants to receive from them his share of the harvest. ³ The tenants seized the slave, beat him, and sent him back without a thing. ⁴ Then the owner sent another slave; the tenants beat him over the head and treated him shamefully. ⁵ The owner sent another slave, and they killed him; and they treated many others the same way, beating some and killing others. ⁶ The only one left to send was the man's own dear son. Last of all, then, he sent his son to the tenants. 'I am sure they will respect my son,' he said. ⁷ But those tenants said to one another, 'This is the owner's son. Come on, let's kill him, and his property will be ours!' ⁸ So they seized the son and killed him and threw his body out of the vineyard.

⁹ "What, then, will the owner of the vineyard do?" asked Jesus. "He will come and kill those tenants and hand the vineyard over to others. ¹⁰ Surely you have read this scripture:

'The stone which the builders rejected as worthless
   turned out to be the most important of all.

¹¹ This was done by the Lord;
    what a wonderful sight it is!' "

¹² The Jewish leaders tried to arrest Jesus, because they knew that he had told this parable against them. But they were afraid of the crowd, so they left him and went away.

The Question about Paying Taxes

¹³ Some Pharisees and some members of Herod's party were sent to Jesus to trap him with questions. ¹⁴ They came to him and said, "Teacher, we know that you tell the truth, without worrying about what people think. You pay no attention to anyone's status, but teach the truth about God's will for people. Tell us, is it against our Law to pay taxes to the Roman Emperor? Should we pay them or not?"

¹⁵ But Jesus saw through their trick and answered, "Why are you trying to trap me? Bring a silver coin, and let me see it."

¹⁶ They brought him one, and he asked, "Whose face and name are these?"

"The Emperor's," they answered.

¹⁷ So Jesus said, "Well, then, pay the Emperor what belongs to the Emperor, and pay God what belongs to God."

And they were amazed at Jesus.

The Question about Rising from Death

[18] Then some Sadducees, who say that people will not rise from death, came to Jesus and said, [19] "Teacher, Moses wrote this law for us: 'If a man dies and leaves a wife but no children, that man's brother must marry the widow so that they can have children who will be considered the dead man's children.' [20] Once there were seven brothers; the eldest got married and died without having children. [21] Then the second one married the woman, and he also died without having children. The same thing happened to the third brother, [22] and then to the rest: all seven brothers married the woman and died without having children. Last of all, the woman died. [23] Now, when all the dead rise to life on the day of resurrection, whose wife will she be? All seven of them had married her."

[24] Jesus answered them, "How wrong you are! And do you know why? It is because you don't know the Scriptures or God's power. [25] For when the dead rise to life, they will be like the angels in heaven and will not marry. [26] Now, as for the dead being raised: haven't you ever read in the Book of Moses the passage about the burning bush? There it is written that God said to Moses, 'I am the God of Abraham, the God of Isaac, and the God of Jacob.' [27] He is the God of the living, not of the dead. You are completely wrong!"

The Great Commandment

²⁸ A teacher of the Law was there who heard the discussion. He saw that Jesus had given the Sadducees a good answer, so he came to him with a question: "Which commandment is the most important of all?"

²⁹ Jesus replied, "The most important one is this: 'Listen, Israel! The Lord our God is the only Lord. ᵃ ³⁰ Love the Lord your God with all your heart, with all your soul, with all your mind, and with all your strength.' ³¹ The second most important commandment is this: 'Love your neighbour as you love yourself.' There is no other commandment more important than these two."

³² The teacher of the Law said to Jesus, "Well done, Teacher! It is true, as you say, that only the Lord is God and that there is no other god but he. ³³ And to love God with all your heart and with all your mind and with all your strength, and to love your neighbour as yourself, is more important than to offer animals and other sacrifices to God."

³⁴ Jesus noticed how wise his answer was, and so he told him, "You are not far from the Kingdom of God."

After this nobody dared to ask Jesus any more questions.

---

a 12.29 The Lord our God is the only Lord; *or* The Lord is our God, the Lord alone.

The Question about the Messiah

[35] As Jesus was teaching in the Temple, he asked the question, "How can the teachers of the Law say that the Messiah will be the descendant of David? [36] The Holy Spirit inspired David to say:

'The Lord said to my Lord:

Sit here on my right

until I put your enemies under your feet.'

[37] David himself called him 'Lord'; so how can the Messiah be David's descendant?"

Jesus Warns against the Teachers of the Law

A large crowd was listening to Jesus gladly. [38] As he taught them, he said, "Watch out for the teachers of the Law, who like to walk around in their long robes and be greeted with respect in the market place, [39] who choose the reserved seats in the synagogues and the best places at feasts. [40] They take advantage of widows and rob them of their homes, and then make a show of saying long prayers. Their punishment will be all the worse!"

The Widow's Offering

[41] As Jesus sat near the temple treasury, he watched the people as they dropped in their money. Many rich men dropped in a lot of money; [42] then a poor widow came along and dropped in two little copper coins, worth

about a penny. ⁴³ He called his disciples together and said to them, "I tell you that this poor widow put more in the offering box than all the others. ⁴⁴ For the others put in what they had to spare of their riches; but she, poor as she is, put in all she had – she gave all she had to live on."

Jesus Speaks of the Destruction of the Temple

13 As Jesus was leaving the Temple, one of his disciples said, "Look, Teacher! What wonderful stones and buildings!"

² Jesus answered, "You see these great buildings? Not a single stone here will be left in its place; every one of them will be thrown down."

Troubles and Persecutions

³ Jesus was sitting on the Mount of Olives, across from the Temple, when Peter, James, John, and Andrew came to him in private. ⁴ "Tell us when this will be," they said, "and tell us what will happen to show that the time has come for all these things to take place."

⁵ Jesus said to them, "Be on guard, and don't let anyone deceive you. ⁶ Many men, claiming to speak for me, will come and say, 'I am he!' and they will deceive many people. ⁷ And don't be troubled when you hear the noise of battles close by and news of battles far away. Such things must happen, but they do not mean that the end

has come. [8] Countries will fight each other; kingdoms will attack one another. There will be earthquakes everywhere, and there will be famines. These things are like the first pains of childbirth.

[9] "You yourselves must be on guard. You will be arrested and taken to court. You will be beaten in the synagogues; you will stand before rulers and kings for my sake to tell them the Good News. [10] But before the end comes, the gospel must be preached to all peoples. [11] And when you are arrested and taken to court, do not worry beforehand about what you are going to say; when the time comes, say whatever is then given to you. For the words you speak will not be yours; they will come from the Holy Spirit. [12] Men will hand over their own brothers to be put to death, and fathers will do the same to their children. Children will turn against their parents and have them put to death. [13] Everyone will hate you because of me. But whoever holds out to the end will be saved.

The Awful Horror

[14] "You will see 'The Awful Horror' standing in the place where he should not be." (Note to the reader: be sure to understand what this means!) "Then those who are in Judea must run away to the hills. [15] Someone who is on the roof of his house must not lose time by going down into the house to get anything to take with him.

¹⁶ Some-one who is in the field must not go back to the house for his cloak. ¹⁷ How terrible it will be in those days for women who are pregnant and for mothers with little babies! ¹⁸ Pray to God that these things will not happen in the winter! ¹⁹ For the trouble of those days will be far worse than any the world has ever known from the very beginning when God created the world until the present time. Nor will there ever be anything like it again. ²⁰ But the Lord has reduced the number of those days; if he had not, nobody would survive. For the sake of his chosen people, however, he has reduced those days.

²¹ "Then, if anyone says to you, 'Look, here is the Messiah!' or 'Look, there he is!' – do not believe him. ²² For false Messiahs and false prophets will appear. They will perform miracles and wonders in order to deceive even God's chosen people, if possible. ²³ Be on your guard! I have told you everything before the time comes.

The Coming of the Son of Man

²⁴ "In the days after that time of trouble the sun will grow dark, the moon will no longer shine, ²⁵ the stars will fall from heaven, and the powers in space will be driven from their courses. ²⁶ Then the Son of Man will appear, coming in the clouds with great power and glory. ²⁷ He will send the angels out to the four corners of the earth to gather God's chosen people from one end of the world to the other.

The Lesson of the Fig Tree

28 "Let the fig tree teach you a lesson. When its branches become green and tender and it starts putting out leaves, you know that summer is near. 29 In the same way, when you see these things happening, you will know that the time is near, ready to begin. a 30 Remember that all these things will happen before the people now living have all died. 31 Heaven and earth will pass away, but my words will never pass away.

No one Knows the Day or Hour

32 "No one knows, however, when that day or hour will come – neither the angels in heaven, nor the Son; only the Father knows. 33 Be on watch, be alert, for you do not know when the time will come. 34 It will be like a man who goes away from home on a journey and leaves his servants in charge, after giving to each one his own work to do and after telling the doorkeeper to keep watch. 35 Be on guard, then, because you do not know when the master of the house is coming – it might be in the evening or at midnight or before dawn or at sunrise. 36 If he comes suddenly, he must not find you asleep. 37 What I say to you, then, I say to all: watch!"

a 13.29 the time is near, ready to begin; *or* he is near, ready to come.

The Plot against Jesus

14 It was now two days before the Festival of Passover and Unleavened Bread. The chief priests and the teachers of the Law were looking for a way to arrest Jesus secretly and put him to death. ² "We must not do it during the festival," they said, "or the people might riot."

Jesus is Anointed at Bethany

³ Jesus was in Bethany at the house of Simon, a man who had suffered from a dreaded skin disease. While Jesus was eating, a woman came in with an alabaster jar full of a very expensive perfume made of pure nard. She broke the jar and poured the perfume on Jesus' head. ⁴ Some of the people there became angry and said to one another, "What was the use of wasting the perfume? ⁵ It could have been sold for more than three hundred silver coins ᵃ and the money given to the poor!" And they criticized her harshly.

⁶ But Jesus said, "Leave her alone! Why are you bothering her? She has done a fine and beautiful thing for me. ⁷ You will always have poor people with you, and any time you want to, you can help them. But you will not always have me. ⁸ She did what she could; she poured

a 14.5 SILVER COINS: See 6.37.

perfume on my body to prepare it ahead of time for burial. ⁹ Now, I assure you that wherever the gospel is preached all over the world, what she has done will be told in memory of her."

Judas Agrees to Betray Jesus

¹⁰ Then Judas Iscariot, one of the twelve disciples, went off to the chief priests in order to betray Jesus to them. ¹¹ They were pleased to hear what he had to say, and promised to give him money. So Judas started looking for a good chance to hand Jesus over to them.

Jesus Eats the Passover Meal with his Disciples

¹² On the first day of the Festival of Unleavened Bread, the day the lambs for the Passover meal were killed, Jesus' disciples asked him, "Where do you want us to go and get the Passover meal ready for you?"

¹³ Then Jesus sent two of them with these instructions: "Go into the city, and a man carrying a jar of water will meet you. Follow him ¹⁴ to the house he enters, and say to the owner of the house: 'The Teacher says, Where is the room where my disciples and I will eat the Passover meal?' ¹⁵ Then he will show you a large upstairs room, prepared and furnished, where you will get everything ready for us."

¹⁶ The disciples left, went to the city, and found

everything just as Jesus had told them; and they prepared the Passover meal.

¹⁷ When it was evening, Jesus came with the twelve disciples. ¹⁸ While they were at the table eating, Jesus said, "I tell you that one of you will betray me – one who is eating with me."

¹⁹ The disciples were upset and began to ask him, one after the other, "Surely you don't mean me, do you?"

²⁰ Jesus answered, "It will be one of you twelve, one who dips his bread in the dish with me. ²¹ The Son of Man will die as the Scriptures say he will; but how terrible for that man who betrays the Son of Man! It would have been better for that man if he had never been born!"

The Lord's Supper

²² While they were eating, Jesus took a piece of bread, gave a prayer of thanks, broke it, and gave it to his disciples. "Take it," he said, "this is my body."

²³ Then he took a cup, gave thanks to God, and handed it to them; and they all drank from it. ²⁴ Jesus said, "This is my blood which is poured out for many, my blood which seals God's covenant. ²⁵ I tell you, I will never again drink this wine until the day I drink the new wine in the Kingdom of God."

²⁶ Then they sang a hymn and went out to the Mount of Olives.

Jesus Predicts Peter's Denial

²⁷ Jesus said to them, "All of you will run away and leave me, for the scripture says, 'God will kill the shepherd, and the sheep will all be scattered.' ²⁸ But after I am raised to life, I will go to Galilee ahead of you."

²⁹ Peter answered, "I will never leave you, even though all the rest do!"

³⁰ Jesus said to Peter, "I tell you that before the cock crows twice tonight, you will say three times that you do not know me."

³¹ Peter answered even more strongly, "I will never say that, even if I have to die with you!"

And all the other disciples said the same thing.

Jesus Prays in Gethsemane

³² They came to a place called Gethsemane, and Jesus said to his disciples, "Sit here while I pray." ³³ He took Peter, James, and John with him. Distress and anguish came over him, ³⁴ and he said to them, "The sorrow in my heart is so great that it almost crushes me. Stay here and keep watch."

³⁵ He went a little farther on, threw himself on the ground, and prayed that, if possible, he might not have to go through that time of suffering. ³⁶ "Father," he prayed, "my Father! All things are possible for you. Take this cup of suffering away from me. Yet not what I want, but what you want."

[37] Then he returned and found the three disciples asleep. He said to Peter, "Simon, are you asleep? Weren't you able to stay awake even for one hour?" [38] And he said to them, "Keep watch, and pray that you will not fall into temptation. The spirit is willing, but the flesh is weak."

[39] He went away once more and prayed, saying the same words. [40] Then he came back to the disciples and found them asleep; they could not keep their eyes open. And they did not know what to say to him.

[41] When he came back the third time, he said to them, "Are you still sleeping and resting? Enough! The hour has come! Look, the Son of Man is now being handed over to the power of sinners. [42] Get up, let us go. Look, here is the man who is betraying me!"

The Arrest of Jesus

[43] Jesus was still speaking when Judas, one of the twelve disciples, arrived. With him was a crowd armed with swords and clubs, and sent by the chief priests, the teachers of the Law, and the elders. [44] The traitor had given the crowd a signal: "The man I kiss is the one you want. Arrest him and take him away under guard."

[45] As soon as Judas arrived, he went up to Jesus and said, "Teacher!" and kissed him. [46] So they arrested Jesus and held him tight. [47] But one of those standing there drew his sword and struck at the High Priest's slave,

cutting off his ear. [48] Then Jesus spoke up and said to them, "Did you have to come with swords and clubs to capture me, as though I were an outlaw? [49] Day after day I was with you teaching in the Temple, and you did not arrest me. But the Scriptures must come true."

[50] Then all the disciples left him and ran away.

[51] A certain young man, dressed only in a linen cloth, was following Jesus. They tried to arrest him, [52] but he ran away naked, leaving the cloth behind.

Jesus before the Council

[53] Then Jesus was taken to the High Priest's house, where all the chief priests, the elders, and the teachers of the Law were gathering. [54] Peter followed from a distance and went into the courtyard of the High Priest's house. There he sat down with the guards, keeping himself warm by the fire. [55] The chief priests and the whole Council tried to find some evidence against Jesus in order to put him to death, but they could not find any. [56] Many witnesses told lies against Jesus, but their stories did not agree.

[57] Then some men stood up and told this lie against Jesus: [58] "We heard him say, 'I will tear down this Temple which men have made, and after three days I will build one that is not made by men.'" [59] Not even they, however, could make their stories agree.

[60] The High Priest stood up in front of them all and questioned Jesus, "Have you no answer to the accusation they bring against you?"

[61] But Jesus kept quiet and would not say a word. Again the High Priest questioned him, "Are you the Messiah, the Son of the Blessed God?"

[62] "I am," answered Jesus, "and you will all see the Son of Man seated on the right of the Almighty and coming with the clouds of heaven!"

[63] The High Priest tore his robes and said, "We don't need any more witnesses! [64] You heard his blasphemy. What is your decision?"

They all voted against him: he was guilty and should be put to death.

[65] Some of them began to spit on Jesus, and they blindfolded him and hit him. "Guess who hit you!" they said. And the guards took him and slapped him.

Peter Denies Jesus

[66] Peter was still down in the courtyard when one of the High Priest's servant women came by. [67] When she saw Peter warming himself, she looked straight at him and said, "You, too, were with Jesus of Nazareth."

[68] But he denied it. "I don't know ... I don't understand what you are talking about," he answered, and

went out into the passage. Just then a cock crowed. [a]

[69] The servant woman saw him there and began to repeat to the bystanders, "He is one of them!" [70] But Peter denied it again.

A little while later the bystanders accused Peter again, "You can't deny that you are one of them, because you, too, are from Galilee."

[71] Then Peter said, "I swear that I am telling the truth! May God punish me if I am not! I do not know the man you are talking about!"

[72] Just then a cock crowed a second time, and Peter remembered how Jesus had said to him, "Before the cock crows twice, you will say three times that you do not know me." And he broke down and cried.

Jesus is Brought before Pilate

15 Early in the morning the chief priests met hurriedly with the elders, the teachers of the Law, and the whole Council, and made their plans. They put Jesus in chains, led him away, and handed him over to Pilate. [2] Pilate questioned him, "Are you the king of the Jews?"

Jesus answered, "So you say."

[3] The chief priests were accusing Jesus of many things,

---

a 14.68 *Some manuscripts do not have* Just then a cock crowed.

[4] so Pilate questioned him again, "Aren't you going to answer? Listen to all their accusations!"

[5] Again Jesus refused to say a word, and Pilate was amazed.

Jesus is Sentenced to Death

[6] At every Passover Festival, Pilate was in the habit of setting free any one prisoner the people asked for. [7] At that time a man named Barabbas was in prison with the rebels who had committed murder in the riot. [8] When the crowd gathered and began to ask Pilate for the usual favour, [9] he asked them, "Do you want me to set free for you the king of the Jews?" [10] He knew very well that the chief priests had handed Jesus over to him because they were jealous.

[11] But the chief priests stirred up the crowd to ask, instead, for Pilate to set Barabbas free for them. [12] Pilate spoke again to the crowd, "What, then, do you want me to do with the one you call the king of the Jews?"

[13] They shouted back, "Crucify him!"

[14] "But what crime has he committed?" Pilate asked.

They shouted all the louder, "Crucify him!"

[15] Pilate wanted to please the crowd, so he set Barabbas free for them. Then he had Jesus whipped and handed him over to be crucified.

The Soldiers Mock Jesus

[16] The soldiers took Jesus inside to the courtyard of the governor's palace and called together the rest of the company. [17] They put a purple robe on Jesus, made a crown out of thorny branches, and put it on his head. [18] Then they began to salute him: "Long live the King of the Jews!" [19] They beat him over the head with a stick, spat on him, fell on their knees, and bowed down to him. [20] When they had finished mocking him, they took off the purple robe and put his own clothes back on him. Then they led him out to crucify him.

Jesus is Crucified

[21] On the way they met a man named Simon, who was coming into the city from the country, and the soldiers forced him to carry Jesus' cross. (Simon was from Cyrene and was the father of Alexander and Rufus.) [22] They took Jesus to a place called Golgotha, which means "The Place of the Skull". [23] There they tried to give him wine mixed with a drug called myrrh, but Jesus would not drink it. [24] Then they crucified him and divided his clothes among themselves, throwing dice to see who would get which piece of clothing. [25] It was nine o'clock in the morning when they crucified him. [26] The notice of the accusation against him said: "The King of the Jews". [27] They also

crucified two bandits with Jesus, one on his right and the other on his left. [a]

²⁹ People passing by shook their heads and hurled insults at Jesus: "Aha! You were going to tear down the Temple and build it up again in three days! ³⁰ Now come down from the cross and save yourself!"

³¹ In the same way the chief priests and the teachers of the Law jeered at Jesus, saying to each other, "He saved others, but he cannot save himself! ³² Let us see the Messiah, the king of Israel, come down from the cross now, and we will believe in him!"

And the two who were crucified with Jesus insulted him also.

The Death of Jesus

³³ At noon the whole country was covered with darkness, which lasted for three hours. ³⁴ At three o'clock Jesus cried out with a loud shout, *"Eloi, Eloi, lema sabachthani?"* which means, "My God, my God, why did you abandon me?"

³⁵ Some of the people there heard him and said, "Listen, he is calling for Elijah!" ³⁶ One of them ran up with a sponge, soaked it in cheap wine, and put it on the

a 15.27 *Some manuscripts add verse 28:* In this way the scripture came true which says, "He shared the fate of criminals" *(see Lk 22.37).*

end of a stick. Then he held it up to Jesus' lips and said, "Wait! Let us see if Elijah is coming to bring him down from the cross!"

[37] With a loud cry Jesus died.

[38] The curtain hanging in the Temple was torn in two, from top to bottom. [39] The army officer who was standing there in front of the cross saw how Jesus had died. [a] "This man was really the Son of God!" he said.

[40] Some women were there, looking on from a distance. Among them were Mary Magdalene, Mary the mother of the younger James and of Joseph, and Salome. [41] They had followed Jesus while he was in Galilee and had helped him. Many other women who had come to Jerusalem with him were there also.

The Burial of Jesus

[42–43] It was towards evening when Joseph of Arimathea arrived. He was a respected member of the Council, who was waiting for the coming of the Kingdom of God. It was Preparation day (that is, the day before the Sabbath), so Joseph went boldly into the presence of Pilate and asked him for the body of Jesus. [44] Pilate was surprised to hear that Jesus was already dead. He called the army officer and asked him if Jesus had been dead a long time.

a 15.39 had died; *some manuscripts have* had cried out and died.

⁴⁵ After hearing the officer's report, Pilate told Joseph he could have the body. ⁴⁶ Joseph bought a linen sheet, took the body down, wrapped it in the sheet, and placed it in a tomb which had been dug out of solid rock. Then he rolled a large stone across the entrance to the tomb. ⁴⁷ Mary Magdalene and Mary the mother of Joseph were watching and saw where the body of Jesus was placed.

The Resurrection

16 After the Sabbath was over, Mary Magdalene, Mary the mother of James, and Salome bought spices to go and anoint the body of Jesus. ² Very early on Sunday morning, at sunrise, they went to the tomb. ³⁻⁴ On the way they said to one another, "Who will roll away the stone for us from the entrance to the tomb?" (It was a very large stone.) Then they looked up and saw that the stone had already been rolled back. ⁵ So they entered the tomb, where they saw a young man sitting on the right, wearing a white robe – and they were alarmed.

⁶ "Don't be alarmed," he said. "I know you are looking for Jesus of Nazareth, who was crucified. He is not here – he has been raised! Look, here is the place where they put him. ⁷ Now go and give this message to his disciples, including Peter: 'He is going to Galilee ahead of you; there you will see him, just as he told you.' "

[8] So they went out and ran from the tomb, distressed and terrified. They said nothing to anyone, because they were afraid.

An Old Ending to the Gospel [a]
16.9–20

Jesus Appears to Mary Magdalene
[[9] After Jesus rose from death early on Sunday, he appeared first to Mary Magdalene, from whom he had driven out seven demons. [10] She went and told his companions. They were mourning and crying; [11] and when they heard her say that Jesus was alive and that she had seen him, they did not believe her.

Jesus Appears to Two Disciples
[12] After this, Jesus appeared in a different manner to two of them while they were on their way to the country. [13] They returned and told the others, but they would not believe it.

Jesus Appears to the Eleven
[14] Last of all, Jesus appeared to the eleven disciples as

a 16.9–20 heading *Some manuscripts and ancient translations do not have this ending to the Gospel (verses 9–20).*

they were eating. He scolded them, because they did not have faith and because they were too stubborn to believe those who had seen him alive. [15] He said to them, "Go throughout the whole world and preach the gospel to the whole human race. [16] Whoever believes and is baptized will be saved; whoever does not believe will be condemned. [17] Believers will be given the power to perform miracles: they will drive out demons in my name; they will speak in strange tongues; [18] if they pick up snakes or drink any poison, they will not be harmed; they will place their hands on sick people, who will get well."

Jesus is Taken Up to Heaven

[19] After the Lord Jesus had talked with them, he was taken up to heaven and sat at the right side of God. [20] The disciples went and preached everywhere, and the Lord worked with them and proved that their preaching was true by the miracles that were performed.]

Another Old Ending [a]
16.9–10

[[9] The women went to Peter and his friends and gave them a brief account of all they had been told. [10] After this, Jesus himself sent out through his disciples from the east to the west the sacred and ever-living message of eternal salvation.]

---

a 16.9–10 heading *Some manuscripts and ancient translations have this shorter ending to the Gospel in addition to the longer ending (verses 9–20).*

Also available in the same series:

LIFELINES

edited by Chris Gidney

The Story of Russell Boulter

I read the Gospels as I would have read a novel, and frankly I was shocked! The Jesus I was told about at school wore a nightie and floated a few feet above the ground. But this Jesus was dangerous and exciting.

Russell Boulter is better known as Detective Sergeant Boulton in *The Bill*. When an uncle gave him a Bible, Russell was overcome with embarrassment. He read it in secret by torchlight, but he was amazed by what he found. He thought all Christians were "dorks" but Jesus was very different and Russell couldn't help liking him – which was a problem as he was an atheist at the time.

This *Lifelines* book introduces TV actor Russell Boulter, who finds a faith he can believe in. Russell's story is followed by the story which astounded him – the Gospel of Mark.